CONTENTS

Foreword

1. **Introduction**
2. **Property and access rights**
   Rights of way and roads 4
   Public access to areas of land 7
   Liability 10
3. **Public highways** 13
   What highways exist? 13
   Records of highways 15
   Resolving uncertainty 21
   Maintenance and protection 28
   Improving the network 36
4. **Providing access by agreement** 47
   New routes 47
   Access to areas of land 49
   Providing for formal activities 54
   Access for those with special needs 57
5. **Management issues and problems** 59
   Dealing with trespass 59
   New Age Travellers 60
   Dogs 60
   Crop spraying 61
   Cycling 62
   Motor vehicles 62
   Promoted routes 64
   Sponsored events or competitions 64
   Gates and stiles 65
   Fences 66
   Litter 66
   Car parking 66
   Shooting and carrying firearms 67
   Poaching and disturbance of wildlife 68
   Metal detecting 69
   Fruit picking 69
   Woodland management 70
   Bulls 70
   Theft 71

Useful publications 72

Useful addresses 75

FOREWORD

Millions of people use our countryside every year as a place of recreation. They enjoy the privilege of walking, riding, cycling or driving through some of the most attractive countryside in the world. It is clear that, as our population grows and new outdoor leisure pursuits gain popularity, the pressure for public access to the countryside will grow. Yet, the same countryside is the work place of farmers producing our food supplies, providing jobs and contributing to the rural economy. The potential for conflict between the various interests is obvious, but avoidable if everyone sticks to the rules.

Many of the problems that do arise result from the lack of understanding or knowledge of the law rather than of any deliberate intention to break it. This booklet is directed primarily at farmers and landowners. It should help them to obtain the answers to their questions about legitimate public access to their land or, at least, to find out where they should look for answers. I commend the Country Landowners' Association, National Farmers' Union and the Countryside Commission for their initiative in preparing this guide. I hope that farmers and landowners will find it useful in helping them to accommodate those who enjoy the use of their land and that their better understanding of the law will contribute to the harmony that we all seek in the countryside.

The Earl Howe
Parliamentary Secretary (Lords)
Ministry of Agriculture, Fisheries and Food

1. INTRODUCTION

The countryside is increasingly valued by residents and visitors alike as a place for recreation and relaxation. This public interest represents a new opportunity for landowners and farmers. For example, several Government schemes now exist to improve public access through voluntary agreements, with payments. Some local authorities are also entering into access agreements. Sports clubs are increasingly seeking suitable sites for many different activities.

Equally, access can sometimes pose problems for landowners and farmers and bring them into conflict with the public. This guide provides basic practical advice to satisfy all interests in seeking solutions to difficult situations. Management holds the key and it is landowners and farmers, the primary land managers, who are often best-placed to take positive action. Practical help is also often available from local authorities.

This guide is not intended to answer every question. Where possible it indicates further sources of information or advice. It is not a substitute for professional advice tailored to specific situations. Care has been taken to ensure that the guide is as accurate as possible but the authors and publishers accept no responsibility for any errors or omissions. This guide is intended to relate only to England. Although the law is the same in Wales, the Countryside Council for Wales will be publishing a similar guide.

Landowners and farmers — 'land managers' in the broadest sense — are the major audience for this guide. The guide will also be made available to local authority staff and the general public. The term 'landowner' is used here to include both the owner-occupier and the landlord. The term 'occupier' includes the owner-occupier and the tenant (on tenanted land).

The Countryside Commission, Country Landowners' Association and National Farmers' Union are grateful to the Ministry of Agriculture, Fisheries and Food for helping to distribute this guide. The authors are also grateful for the constructive criticisms of various individuals expert in access matters. The guide is offered very much as a contribution to continuing efforts to secure greater understanding and cooperation among all those concerned with the English countryside.

2. PROPERTY AND ACCESS RIGHTS

It is very unusual indeed for individual landowners to have absolute control of all the property rights associated with their land. Much depends on what rights, if any, are vested in other people. For example, a mortgagee might have a charge, or a tenant a lease. The utility companies may also hold easements for their pipelines, cables and associated structures.

The rights held by the public over private property, in particular, rights of access over defined routes, or over defined areas of land, are no different in legal terms from the property rights vested in any other person or body. Landowners and farmers exercise their rights to use and manage land subject to all the property rights vested in others.

This chapter focuses on the various property rights vested in landowners and the public. It deals with rights of way and roads (see pages 4–6), public access to areas of land (see pages 7–9), and liability issues (see pages 10–12).

Rights of way and roads

There is a substantial volume of statute law and case law governing access to land over defined routes. Statute law is contained in legislation; case law is either common law (where no statute exists) or a judicial interpretation of legislation in a specific case. Landowners and farmers particularly need to be aware of the status of highways, the laws of trespass and the status of private rights of way.

The status of highways

A 'highway' is a defined route over which the public has a right of access. Public highways are customarily divided into two categories: 'public rights of way' and 'public roads'. Public footpaths and motorways are both highways in law: the difference lies in the ways in which each can be used. Both should be respected by those whose land they cross. Highways must be kept open and available for public use at all times.

Once a highway comes into existence it remains a highway unless and until it is 'stopped-up' or 'extinguished' by a formal legal procedure: it cannot be lost by non-use alone. 'Once a highway, always a highway' is an important maxim. A highway may not be visible on the ground because it has not been used for many years, but that does not alter its legal status, including the obligation to keep it open and available for use.

Where a highway is maintainable at public expense (as most are) the right to control the land is vested in the highway authority, not in the landowner or occupier. In simple terms, the surface of a highway, whether a public right of way or a road, is owned by the highway authority rather than by the owner of the land over which it passes. In some cases the highway authority may also own the subsoil. Obstructing a highway or damaging its surface are criminal offences under the Highways Act 1980.

Trespass

People who stray from highways, or from other land to which the public have a right of access, without permission, commit the civil wrong of trespass. People who cause damage while trespassing may commit a criminal offence (of 'criminal damage') but simple trespass is not a criminal offence. Signs saying "Trespassers will be prosecuted" are misleading; "Trespassers may be sued" would be more accurate. Trespass is only a criminal offence where specific Acts forbid it (eg in relation to railway land).

The public's right over a highway is limited: it has been defined as a "right of passage for the purpose of passing and re-passing and for purposes reasonably incidental thereto". The class of highway legally determines whether it can be used on foot, horseback or bicycle, or in a motor vehicle. Other limitations depend on case law rather than statute. For example, it would be reasonable for a user to take a push-chair on a footpath, or to be accompanied by a dog.

Case law has also determined what users can do on highways. For example, stopping to admire the view, to talk to a passer-by, to take a photograph, to make a sketch, or to eat a simple picnic would be acceptable, so long as no obstruction is caused. Whether an activity is acceptable depends on what a court would regard as reasonable in all the circumstances of the particular case.

Members of the public may trespass inadvertently while seeking to follow existing public rights of way. Trespass of this sort is best avoided by ensuring that the paths are well-defined. Users are permitted to deviate around an obstruction on a public right of way without committing a trespass. In some cases, users considered to be trespassers by the landowner or farmer may strongly maintain that they have a right to use a particular path. In such cases the highway authority should be asked to examine all the evidence so that the situation can be clarified in the interests of all.

Private rights of way

Private rights of way are termed 'easements'. For example, one landowner might have a private right of access over a neighbour's land. This would usually be mentioned in the deeds of both properties. Such private rights should be respected by all parties. Some ways can carry both public and private rights. For example, a farm access road may also be a public bridleway, and a public footpath may also carry private vehicular rights. Private rights must not be exercised in such a way as to interfere with the rights of the public.

Key points: Rights of way and roads

- The public have a right to use highways over private land.
- 'Highway' includes all 'public rights of way' (footpaths, bridleways, byways open to all traffic and 'roads used as public paths') and all 'public roads' (whether surfaced or unsurfaced).
- Highways can only be closed through legal proceedings: they do not cease to exist simply because they are not used or are not apparent on the ground.
- In general the highway authority owns the surface of a publicly-maintainable highway, the landowner owns the subsoil.

Private rights of access can also exist over highways but must not be exercised so as to interfere with public rights.

See pages 72–74 for sources of further information.

Public access to areas of land

Members of the public do not have a general right of access to land in England beyond highways. Access can be provided to areas of land rather than defined routes as a result of specific Acts of Parliament, by the granting of rights by landowners, or by agreement with landowners. The courts have also accepted that residents of an area, but not the general public, can acquire the right to use land for 'lawful sports and pastimes', through a tradition of such use.

The various areas to which formal public access can exist include common land, town and village greens and land covered by access agreements or orders. Long-standing informal public access (*de facto* access) exists in many areas, even though it is not based on any legal right.

Common land

There is considerable confusion about public rights over 'common land'. Many people wrongly believe that common land implies public ownership and that they have a right to wander over it at will. In fact, most common land is private land over which people known as 'commoners' have specific rights of use (eg to graze sheep or cattle, to collect firewood, or to fish). These rights are in addition to those of the owner of the common. Some common land is land that is, or was, 'waste land of a manor' not subject to rights of common.

Common land and common rights must be registered under the Commons Registration Act 1965. County councils hold the registers. Some 7,052 commons, with a total area of 368,800 hectares (911,300 acres) have been registered in England. They cover less than four per cent of the entire area of the country. The largest areas lie in Cumbria, North Yorkshire, Devon and Durham.

The public has a right of access to some, but not all, common land. In particular, there is a right of access to all common land wholly or partly in the area of a former urban or metropolitan district council (under Section 193 of the Law of Property Act 1925). This affects about one-fifth of the total common land area. Some of these commons are rural in nature: for example, there is a right of access to many commons in the Lake District.

Local inhabitants or the general public may also enjoy rights of access over certain rural commons under various Acts and formal management schemes, eg a 'Scheme of Regulation' run by the district council. In practice, the general public often use such land for access without challenge. Owners may also enter into access agreements with local authorities over common land (but they must bear in mind the interests of the registered commoners). Owners may also by deed provide for public access under Section 193 of the Law of Property Act 1925.

Under Section 194 of the 1925 Act, the consent of the Secretary of State for the Environment is required for the construction of any building or fence, or any other work, that interferes with any public rights of access to common land (or private rights, eg those of commoners). This applies to all fences, however 'temporary' they may be, and regardless of their purposes (eg consent is still required for fences to control stock for conservation reasons), unless they are specifically allowed under subsection (4).

New common land can be created where rights of common are granted to commoners by landowners or acquired by prescription (eg use, as of right, for a period of 20 years) over land which is not already common land. Both the rights and the land can then be registered under Section 13 of the Commons Registration Act 1965.

Many problems on commons today result from a lack of coordinated management. Although there is no legislation which requires it, there is much to be gained if owners, commoners and local authorities jointly establish voluntary management associations to promote agreed action. Local user groups should also be involved.

Town and village greens

Town and village greens are areas of land, registered under the Commons Registration Act 1965, that come within the following definition:
- land that has been allotted by or under any Act for the exercise or recreation of the inhabitants of any locality;
- land on which the inhabitants of any locality have a customary right to indulge in lawful sports and pastimes;
- land on which the inhabitants of any locality have indulged in such sports and pastimes as of right for not less than 20 years.

The phrase "lawful sports and pastimes" has never been defined. It has been accepted as including such activities as the village cricket match, maypole dancing, flying a kite and 'idling beside the river'. Some 3,634 town and village greens in England have been registered as such under the Commons Registration Act 1965.

As with common land, new village greens may be claimed on the basis of use, as of right, for a period of 20 years. There have been several such claims in recent years.

Access agreements and orders

Landowners can enter into agreements to provide for public access to land, air and water with local authorities, statutory agencies and Government departments. Chapter 4 gives details of various options, which also include private agreements with user groups.

Local authorities may also make access orders to secure public access over land defined as 'open country' whether or not the landowner is in agreement. The orders need to be confirmed by the Secretary of State for the Environment. Adequate notice must be given to the landowner and compensation must be paid by the authority. Few access orders are in existence. In most cases where they might have been used, access has been secured through an agreement, following negotiations.

De facto access

The public have access to many areas of land to which they have not been specifically invited and to which no formal rights of access apply. Access in these cases is a fact (*de facto*) not a right (*de jure*). In practice, such use is often tolerated, particularly where it is low-key and local people are involved. *De facto* access may also exist simply because it is impractical to prevent or control access to the land involved (eg extensive, remote and unenclosed moorland areas).

Key points: Public access to areas of land

- There is no general right of access to private land adjoining public rights of way or other highways.
- Common land is private land subject to rights of common or waste land of the manor. A right of public access for local inhabitants or the general public exists to about one-fifth of the total area of common land.
- Town and village greens are areas where local people have a customary right of access for lawful sports and pastimes.
- Local authorities may negotiate access agreements with landowners. Exceptionally they may seek access orders over 'open country' where agreements are not possible.
- Many areas of land, particularly in the uplands, are subject to *de facto* public access, rather than formal rights of access.
- See pages 72–74 for sources of further information.

Liability

Landowners and occupiers need to be aware of their duty of care to other people who come on to their land, under both the Occupiers' Liability Acts and other legislation. These duties apply both to visitors, and, in certain circumstances, to trespassers. They also have implications for public liability insurance.

Deciding exactly what duty of care one person owes to another can be a difficult legal question needing the advice of a solicitor. Almost invariably, this will depend on the facts of the individual case, and what the person knew or should have known, in all the circumstances. The following advice should be read with this qualification in mind.

The duty of care

The Occupiers' Liability Act 1957 sets out a duty of care to people who come on to land by invitation of the owner or occupier or who are permitted to be there. The duty is to take care over the state of the land so that visitors (which could include children) will be reasonably safe in using it for the intended or permitted purposes. For example, farmers should take steps to protect the public from hazards such as slurry lagoons.

The Act provides that this duty does not impose any obligation on an owner or occupier to a visitor who willingly accepts risks. This is a statutory enactment of the common law principle *volenti non fit injuria*, (a willing person cannot be injured, ie injured in law).

Climbers and mountain walkers, for example, voluntarily accept the risks of their sport or recreation. If a climber or hill walker is injured in an accident any claim against the owner or occupier is likely to be defeated by the defence that the injured person willingly accepted the risks.

The Occupiers' Liability Act 1984 extends the duty of care to people other than visitors, including trespassers, but only if three conditions are fulfilled: that the owner or occupier knows, or ought to know, of dangers on his or her premises; that he or she knows or suspects that people might come near that danger; and that the risk is one against which he or she might reasonably be expected to offer some protection.

Again, the duty of care does not apply towards a person who willingly accepts a risk. In addition, an owner or occupier may discharge the duty by warning of the danger and discouraging people from taking risks. Warning notices should indicate both the dangers and where the liability lies, for example: "These cliffs are dangerous. Persons who climb on them or go near them must accept risks of injury to themselves and others".

Other relevant legislation

The Mines and Quarries Acts serve mainly to secure the safety, health and welfare of employees at mines and quarries, but some provisions protect other categories of person as well. For example, a quarry manager has a duty to make sure that quarrying operations avoid danger from rock falls. Thus owners of working quarries would be justified in excluding all recreational 'visitors'.

A quarry, whether being worked or not, is deemed to be a statutory nuisance (under Section 151 of the Mines and Quarries Act 1954), and, if it is accessible from a highway or public place, it should be provided with an efficient and properly maintained barrier to prevent persons accidentally falling into it. Similarly the entrance or shaft to an abandoned mine should be efficiently closed off and the closure properly maintained.

The Health and Safety at Work etc. Act 1974 places both employers and the self-employed under a duty to conduct their undertakings so as to avoid risks to others. For example, farmers should try to avoid keeping any aggressive animal in a field crossed by a right of way. There are specific duties in relation to bulls (see page 70). Slurry lagoons, buildings, farm machinery and farming operations (eg spraying of pesticides) may also pose risks.

Liability on defined routes

The surface of a publicly-maintainable highway is vested in the highway authority. It follows that it is the highway authority which is responsible to users of a highway who are injured because the way is in disrepair, not the landowner or occupier. However, a highway authority could take action against a landowner or occupier who had created any source of danger on or near a highway or who had failed to keep back vegetation encroaching on a highway from the sides or above.

On a privately-maintainable highway, or a permitted (or 'permissive') path or toll-ride, it is the landowner or occupier who remains responsible for the surface of the path and who therefore could be held to be liable for any accident. Landowners who wish to establish permitted paths or toll-rides should bear this responsibility in mind, and take out appropriate insurance as necessary. Further information on permitted paths and toll-rides is given on pages 47–48.

Liability insurance

Landowners or occupiers are unlikely to be liable towards visitors on their land who have an accident while engaged in a dangerous sport (eg climbing, hang-gliding, pot-holing). Such visitors willingly accept the risks involved in their sports. However, landowners and occupiers may be liable for any accident occurring while such visitors are gaining access to a site (eg a crag, hill-top or pot-hole). Landowners and occupiers also have wider duties to the public, including trespassers. For these reasons it is advisable for landowners and occupiers to hold appropriate insurance.

Key points: Liability

- Landowners and occupiers have a duty of care under the Occupiers' Liability Acts to people who come onto their land, including trespassers.

- Landowners and occupiers must also safeguard people who come onto their land from sources of danger such as mines and quarries.

- On public rights of way, the liability for injury (eg due to an inadequate surface) normally lies with the highway authority; on permitted routes the liability rests with the landowner.

- Owners should take out or check their public liability insurance to ensure that they have adequate cover.

- See pages 72–74 for sources of further information.

3. PUBLIC HIGHWAYS

This chapter deals with the variety of different highways (see pages 13–15), public records of their existence and status (see pages 15–21) and the steps which can be taken to resolve uncertainty over them (see pages 21–28). It also sets out who is responsible for maintaining highways (see pages 28–36) and outlines how the existing network can be improved in the interests of all (see pages 36–46).

What highways exist?

Getting to grips with 'highways' involves making two important distinctions: between 'public rights of way' and 'public roads'; and between the four different classes of public rights of way. It is also important to understand how these highways came into existence.

Public rights of way

There are estimated to be about 193,000 kilometres (120,000 miles) of public rights of way in England. They are legally classified as footpaths, bridleways, byways open to all traffic and roads used as public paths:

- A **'public footpath'** is a highway over which the right of way is on foot only. It is a civil wrong to ride a bicycle or a horse, on a footpath: the user could be sued by the landowner for trespass or nuisance. It is a criminal offence under Section 34 of the Road Traffic Act 1988 to drive a motorised vehicle on a footpath. There are about 145,000 kilometres (90,000 miles) of public footpaths in England.
- A **'public bridleway'** is a highway over which the right of way is on foot, on a horse, donkey or mule and on a bicycle (including 'mountain bikes'). Cyclists must give way to walkers and riders. A horse, donkey or mule may also be led. There may also be a right to drive animals other than horses. It is a criminal offence to drive a motor vehicle on a bridleway. There are about 40,000 kilometres (25,000 miles) of bridleways in England.
- A **'public byway open to all traffic'** (BOAT) (often simply termed 'byway') is a highway over which the right of way is on foot, horseback or bicycle, or by wheeled vehicles of all kinds including horse-drawn and motorised vehicles. Any such vehicles must be properly taxed and fit for use on public roads. Their drivers must be licensed and insured. Byways open to all traffic differ from roads in that they are primarily used for walking and riding, rather than by vehicles. There are about 3,200 kilometres (2,000 miles) of byways open to all traffic in England.

- Where **'roads used as public paths'** (RUPPs) are still recorded, highway authorities are under a duty to reclassify them as bridleways, byways open to all traffic or footpaths, according to the public rights which already exist over them. In the meantime, they have at least bridleway status. Landowners must be notified of any reclassification proposal. An estimated 4,600 kilometres (4,000 miles) of RUPPs in England remain to be reclassified.

Kit Houghton/CC

Public roads

Public roads include motorways, trunk roads, A, B, and C ('classified') roads, and other minor ('unclassified') roads (which may or may not be surfaced with tarmac or stone). Public roads primarily carry vehicles, but they may also be used by walkers, cyclists and horse riders if the status of the road allows. The term 'green lane' has no legal meaning. It simply describes an unsurfaced path which may or may not also be a highway (eg an unsurfaced public road, byway open to all traffic, bridleway or footpath).

Dedication of public rights of way

Public rights of way can be established by various means. The options include express dedication by landowners, or creation agreements or orders made by highway authorities (see pages 44–45 for further details). In practice, few public rights of way have been created using these procedures. The great majority have simply come into existence through 'deemed dedication' at common law or under the provisions of Section 31 of the Highways Act 1980.

Dedication of a public right of way at common law may be implied where there has been open use 'as of right' in such a way that the owner must have known that the public was claiming a right. Use must be without permission, secrecy, force, or interruption. The length of the enjoyment necessary depends on all the circumstances. In some cases, use for only a year or so may be sufficient to establish a claim. The onus of proof is on the user.

Alternatively, a public right of way can be claimed under the deemed dedication provisions of Section 31 of the Highways Act 1980 where there has been use for 20 years. Again, use must have been without permission, secrecy, force, or interruption. Use for such a long time raises the presumption of dedication. The onus is therefore on the owner to show that there was no intention to dedicate.

Information on rebutting claims for deemed dedication at common law, or through the parallel statutory procedures, is provided on pages 24–27.

Key points: What highways exist?

- Public rights of way can be footpaths, bridleways, byways open to all traffic (BOATs) or roads used as public paths (RUPPs).

- Public roads include motorways, trunk roads, classified roads and other minor ('unclassified') roads, which may or may not be surfaced.

- Many public rights of way have come into existence through 'deemed dedication' at common law or under the provisions of the Highways Act 1980.

- See pages 72–74 for sources of further information

Records of highways

Highway authorities (county, metropolitan district councils and outer London Boroughs) maintain two sets of records of highways. 'Definitive maps and statements' prepared under Section 53 of the Wildlife and Countryside Act 1981, record public rights of way. 'Lists of streets maintainable at public expense' prepared under Section 36(6) of the Highways Act 1980, record public rights of way and public roads for which highway authorities are responsible. The lists may also be accompanied by maps (though this is not a legal requirement). Both sets of documents should be available for public inspection free of charge at highway authority offices.

Definitive maps and statements

Definitive maps and statements are extremely important records of public rights of way. They provide conclusive evidence, at the relevant date of the map, of the existence and status of the public rights of way which are shown on them. This means that users can legitimately expect the situation on the ground to reflect precisely what is shown on the maps and statements. Moreover, highway authorities are under a duty to ensure that the rights of way shown on the maps are open and available for use.

Every farm and estate office should have an up-to-date copy of the relevant parts of the map and statement. They need to be examined by all those involved in managing the land: landowners, farm managers, farm or estate workers and contractors. Intending purchasers of land should also ensure that they check the relevant section of the definitive map and statement. Copies of extracts may be available from highway authorities (a fee may be payable). Non-metropolitan district and parish or town councils and some libraries may also hold copies of the definitive map and statement for inspection, but these will not necessarily be up-to-date.

Problems with definitive maps and statements

The duty on highway authorities to survey and record rights of way dates only from 1949. The quality of the information used to produce the initial maps varied considerably, because some surveys were much more thorough than others. A further problem was that landowners were not directly notified of the recording of rights of way over their land (although they were able to inspect and object to completed draft maps). In some areas the whole process of producing the initial definitive map took many years. The regular reviews which were also required were then often inadequate or not carried out.

Definitive maps and statements may be incomplete or inaccurate for several reasons. These include:
- rights of way exist in law but have not yet been recorded on the definitive map. Nevertheless their existence may now be capable of being proved either through evidence of public use for 20 years (or possibly a lesser period under common law) or by means of historic or other documents;
- rights of way may have been wrongly designated (eg as a footpath rather than a bridleway) when the original definitive map (or a subsequent revision) was published, and such errors were not spotted and corrected;
- additional (higher) rights than those recorded on the map may have been acquired by virtue of deemed statutory dedication, arising from public use for 20 years (or possibly a lesser period under common law);

- rights of way shown as 'roads used as public paths' may not yet have been reclassified as bridleways, byways or footpaths as required by Section 54 of the Wildlife and Countryside Act 1981;
- 'legal event orders' to amend the definitive map to show the effect of changes brought about by public path orders (eg to create, divert or extinguish rights of way) or other statutory proceedings, may not have been made;
- until 1983 certain areas of the country (eg the former county boroughs) were not covered by the requirement to prepare definitive maps. Some of these excluded areas still await mapping.

These inadequacies mean that definitive maps should be regarded merely as the starting-point in determining precisely what rights of way exist across an area of land. They are conclusive only in respect of what is recorded on them: this does not exclude, the existence of other rights or of rights of a higher status. For example, a private farm track not shown on the definitive map may nevertheless be a public footpath, or a bridleway shown on the definitive map may in fact be a byway open to all traffic. The public may use these additional rights quite legitimately; the problem is that they are simply not recorded. The inadequacies of definitive maps provide a major source of contention between land managers and the public over public rights of way. Highway authorities are making considerable efforts to sort out the problems, but this will take time.

Advice on the steps which landowners can themselves take to resolve uncertainty about public rights of way over their land is given on pages 21–28.

Lists of streets

Definitive maps do not provide information on public roads as such, whether or not they are surfaced. Some highway authorities may consider recording unsurfaced public roads on definitive maps as byways open to all traffic because they are mainly used by walkers, horse riders and cyclists rather than motor vehicles. The existence of vehicular rights over any ways shown as roads used as public paths will be confirmed only where they are reclassified as byways open to all traffic.

A potential source of information about the existence of public roads, whether or not they are surfaced, may be the lists of streets maintainable at public expense. These are also held by highway authorities, under Section 36(6) of the Highways Act 1980. They should show all public rights of way and public roads which are publicly maintainable. In some cases the minor ('unclassified') public roads shown on the lists may no longer be visible on the ground. Such highways are likely to carry vehicular rights. This applies regardless of their current condition.

Example of a definitive map

The figure opposite shows an example of a definitive map, drawn to a scale of 1:10,000 (other maps may be to a smaller scale of $2^1/_2$" to 1 mile). Note that each public right of way is numbered and that there are distinctive markings for each type. The extract also illustrates many of the problems with definitive maps. Note, for example:

- Paths 11, 15 and 30 are still shown as roads used as public paths (RUPPs) and have yet to be reclassified to clarify the rights that exist over them.

- The track from Turnpike Cross to Home Cottage and the path off it through Littleworth Wood are on the base map (ie they are shown as features that exist on the ground) but are not on the definitive map as public rights of way. Their status will need to be checked with the highway authority. (In fact the track is an unclassified public road, and the path is a public right of way that has been missed off the definitive map).

- Path 3 in the centre of the map is shown as a footpath, but seems to be part of a continuous route with RUPPs 15 and 30, suggesting that it might have been wrongly designated. This apparent anomaly should also be checked with the highway authority. (In fact all three paths, 3, 15 and 30, are part of an old carriage route which can legally be used by vehicles. They should all be properly recorded on the definitive map as byways open to all traffic).

The statement which accompanies the map (not shown here) will describe the paths. Many do so only in outline, but some include important information on the position and width of paths and on legal limitations on public use, such as gates and stiles. Where such details are given they are also conclusive evidence in law.

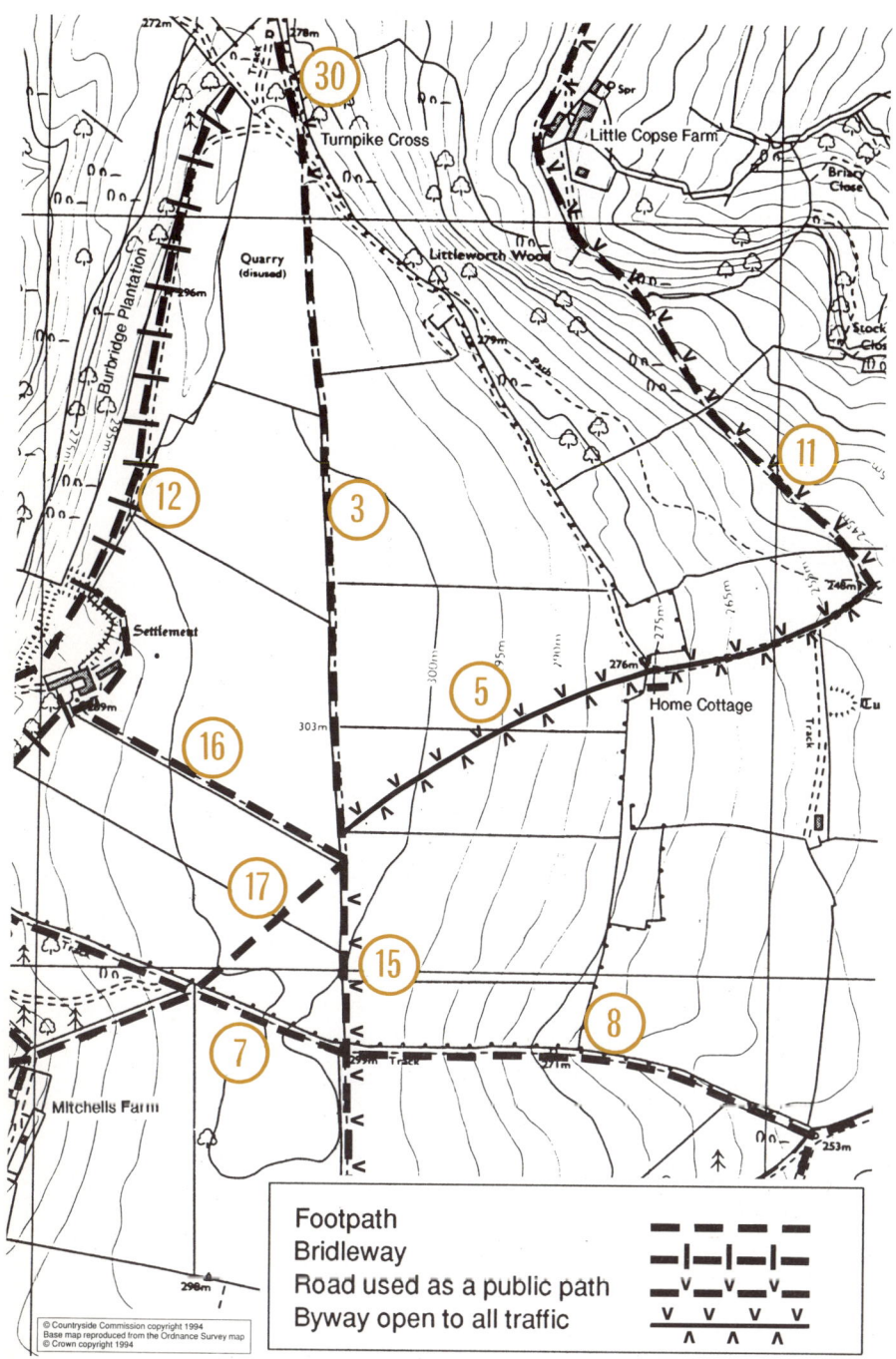

Ordnance Survey maps

Information on public rights of way has been shown on Ordnance Survey (OS) maps in the Landranger, Pathfinder and Outdoor Leisure series for many years. The maps are widely used by members of the public (though by no means all users). Users often expect the maps to be accurate, and to be able to use the rights of way shown on them. Many users plan extensive circular walks, rides or drives using OS maps. Often the aim is to maximise the off-road proportion of the route.

The OS maps which show rights of way always carry a disclaimer to the effect that "representation on this map of any **other** road, track or path is no evidence of the existence of a right of way". However, it does not follow that rights do not exist over such roads, tracks or paths. While OS maps are useful as a general guide, they should therefore not be relied upon as a substitute for the definitive map.

Because OS maps simply repeat what is shown on definitive maps (so far as the limitations of scale allow), they too may be incomplete and inaccurate. A major problem is the time interval between the publication of new editions of OS maps. The information on them can often be many years out-of-date.

Key points: Records of highways

- Find out what public rights of way cross your land by checking the definitive map and statement. Also check the list of streets for any publicly maintainable roads across your land.

- Keep a map showing public rights of way handy, for example in your farm office. Make sure everyone connected with your business or property knows too. (Don't forget tractor drivers, stockmen and contractors as well as tenants).

- Check public rights of way and public roads across your land on the ground yourself. Waymark them to avoid trespass. Remove any obstructions.

- Some highways are still recorded as roads used as public paths (RUPPs). These are gradually being reclassified by local authorities either as byways open to all traffic (BOATs) (if vehicular rights are shown to exist), as footpaths (if bridleway rights are shown not to exist) or otherwise as bridleways. In the meantime, they have at least bridleway status. You should be notified of any reclassification proposal.

- When purchasing new property make sure your solicitor asks the local authority to check the definitive map and statement when undertaking a search of local land charges. This should reveal recorded public rights of way. Further research may be needed to establish whether other ways, or ways of a higher status, exist but have not yet been recorded.

- Users may consider that they have a right to use a route not shown as a right of way, or they have higher rights than those recorded. The best approach in such circumstances is to ask them to provide a copy of their evidence and to discuss it with the highway authority, so that the question of the existence of the rights can be settled.

- If you believe an Ordnance Survey map is wrong, you should check it against the definitive map and statement. You should ask the highway authority to refer any discrepancies to the Ordnance Survey and to ensure that the correct routes are clearly marked on the ground.

- See pages 72–74 for sources of further information.

Resolving uncertainty

There are three main ways in which current uncertainty over the existence and status of rights of way can be resolved. Firstly, anyone can seek an order to modify the definitive map and statement. Secondly, landowners may submit a map, statement and statutory declaration to the highway authority setting out what public rights of way, if any, they recognise over their land. Thirdly, highway authorities are under a duty to keep the definitive map and statement under review and to reclassify any ways shown on the definitive map as roads used as public paths. In each case, factual evidence holds the key. This section summarises the procedures and considerations involved.

Definitive map modification orders

Any landowner, occupier or user can seek an order to modify the definitive map. Landowners and occupiers may believe, for example, that a right of way should never have been shown on the definitive map at all, or is shown on the wrong line, or is incorrectly shown as a bridleway instead of a footpath. Likewise, users may believe that rights of way should be added on the basis of evidence from historical documents, or evidence of use (either over 20 years through deemed statutory dedication, or over possibly a lesser period at common law). Highway authorities must make orders where they discover evidence that shows the definitive map or statement are wrong.

Whoever seeks a definitive map modification order, the same basic principles apply. The most important of these is the need for factual evidence. The whole exercise is concerned with resolving uncertainty over what rights **already** exist, not over what rights are **desirable** from either the public or private viewpoint. Because of this, none of the costs associated with making and confirming a definitive map modification order are charged to the applicant. Different procedures — public path orders — are available where a change is considered desirable, and for which the applicant may be expected to bear some of the costs (see pages 36–46).

This distinction can be illustrated by an example. Suppose that the definitive map shows a public footpath running down one side of a hedgerow. The map can be changed, so as to show the path running down the other side of the hedgerow, in two ways:

- if the map is **wrong**, because evidence shows that the rights actually exist on the other side of the hedgerow, then the highway authority have a duty to make a **definitive map modification order**: the authority would need to have factual documentary evidence, or evidence of use, to make such an order;
- if it is recognised that the rights exist along the current line, but thought that moving the path to the other side of the hedgerow would be **desirable**, then the local authority may be persuaded to make a **public path diversion order**. The authority would need to be satisfied that the proposal meets the legal tests relating to both the private and public interest, and may require the applicant to meet at least part of the costs.

Anyone seeking to have the definitive map altered needs to gather sufficient evidence to persuade a highway authority that, on the balance of probabilities, a definitive map modification order should be made. Evidence can be of two main types: documentary evidence, or evidence based on use. Both types of evidence are often submitted, in various combinations.

Section 32 of the Highways Act 1980 provides for "any map, plan or history of the locality or other relevant documents" to be tendered in evidence of the existence or status of a public right of way. Commonly-used sources include: Inclosure (or Enclosure) awards and maps; Increment Value Duty Records (deriving from the Finance Act 1910); and Tithe awards and maps.

Evidence of use is typically submitted on 'user evidence forms'. Users are asked to define the line of the alleged right of way and to indicate over what period they have used it.

Once sufficient factual evidence has been gathered, the authority can be formally requested to make a definitive map modification order under Sections 53 - 58 of the Wildlife and Countryside Act 1981. When an application is received, the authority must follow a set procedure:

(a) Before making a definitive map modification order, the authority must consult every local authority in the area affected. It may also consult several other organisations, including parish councils and user groups.

(b) Most authorities will also consult landowners and occupiers if an application will affect them, but they are not obliged by law to do so.

(c) The onus is on the applicant to serve notice on landowners and occupiers where applications will affect them.

(d) Having considered the evidence available, an authority may decide to **make** a modification order.

(e) Making the order is only the start of the procedure and no changes are actually made to the map until the order is **confirmed**.

(f) The order will be advertised and a period of at least six weeks allowed for any objections to be submitted.

(g) During this time, anyone may ask the authority to tell them what documents were taken into account in deciding to make the order and either to allow them to be inspected or copied, or to tell them where they can be inspected. It must comply with this duty within 14 days of being asked.

(h)   If no objections are submitted, (or objections are made but later withdrawn) the order may be **confirmed** by the authority and the amendment will then be made to the map and statement accordingly.

(i)   If objections are not withdrawn, the order and the objections will be considered by an independent Inspector on behalf of the Secretary of State for the Environment.

(j)   The Inspector will consider all the evidence given in written representations, or at a public inquiry, before reaching a decision on whether or not to confirm the order.

A more detailed explanation is given in A *guide to definitive map procedures* (CCP 285), published by the Countryside Commission.

Rebutting deemed dedication

Many of the applications made to highway authorities for definitive map modification orders relate to claims based solely on use by the public. These can be lodged under the provisions of the Highways Act 1980 relating to deemed dedication (use for at least 20 years), or at common law (use for possibly a lesser period).

Section 31(6) of the Highways Act 1980 enables landowners to protect themselves against claims based solely on use, by depositing a map, statement and statutory declaration with the highway authority showing which rights of way they acknowledge over their land. All landowners should deposit these documents, not only in their interests, but also in the interests of providing greater certainty for users.

The basic procedure which landowners should adopt in depositing a map, statement and statutory declaration under Section 31 (6) is as follows:

(a)   Obtain a recent or current map at 1:10,000 scale of the entire area involved.

(b)   Examine the definitive map and statement held by the highway authority to ascertain what public rights of way are already recorded, and their precise routes.

(c)   Carefully mark up on the map the precise route of all public rights of way shown on the definitive map, or otherwise acknowledged to exist.

(d)   Do not try to deny the existence of any public rights of way shown on the definitive map unless an application for a definitive map modification order has already been made.

(e) Do not show unofficial diversions: the effect of the statutory declaration will be to confer right of way status on such routes. The route on the definitive map will still remain a public right of way.

(f) Draw up a statement and statutory declaration. Model forms are available from the CLA and NFU (see pages 72–74). Ensure that the documents are accurate and are declared before a Commissioner for Oaths, solicitor or JP. The statement should be made first and the statutory declaration shortly afterwards.

(g) Submit the statement with the map and statutory declaration to the highway authority. If they have not previously checked the map, they may wish to check it against the definitive map and to clarify any areas of uncertainty.

(h) Subsequent statutory declarations are required at intervals of **no more than six years**, for the map and statement to remain effective. They should be accompanied by further maps as necessary.

(i) Keep copies of maps, statements and declarations with the title deeds for the property or Land or Charge Certificate.

(j) It may be useful to place notices on any tracks which are **not** admitted to be public rights of way, to make it clear that that is the position.

The effect of depositing a map, statement and statutory declaration will be threefold:
- It will be possible to allow continued informal use of farm tracks or access roads (eg by local people), without fear of a public right of way being claimed on the basis of future use from the date of the declaration (always provided that there is no other evidence of an intention to dedicate a public right of way).
- Where a track has been used informally, but for less than 20 years, it will not be possible for a right of way to be claimed through deemed statutory dedication (although a claim at common law might still be possible).
- Any new farm tracks or roads will automatically be protected from the possibility of any claim from the outset.

Other forms of evidence to rebut claims include:

- Documentary evidence which clearly shows that the track involved was never intended to be a public right of way. User evidence over 20 years can override such evidence, for example if an inclosure award dating from 1820 shows that the track was a private road, but users show that it has been used as a public right of way since 1970.

- Notices displayed along the track stating that it is not a public right of way, or, where such a notice has been torn down or defaced, a statement lodged with the highway authority under Section 31(5) of the Highways Act 1980 to the same effect. A notice simply saying "Trespassers will be prosecuted" is misleading and insufficient for the purpose of establishing that the track is not a public right of way.

- Evidence that the track has been closed to the public on at least one day every year within the 20-year period over which use is claimed (eg by locking a gate for the explicit purpose of preventing public access). It is also necessary to show that the public were aware that the track had been closed to them for this reason.

- Evidence that users of the track within the 20-year period over which use is claimed have done so with the permission of the owner. For example, estate workers may have been given verbal or written permission to use the track as a short-cut, to get to work or the church, or to exercise their dogs.

- Evidence that a number of users of the track have been turned back on the grounds that it is not a public right of way, by the owner or his agent (eg a tenant, farm manager or gamekeeper) within the 20-year period over which use is claimed.

None of these types of evidence is in itself as reliable as a map, statement and statutory declaration deposited with the highway authority under Section 31(6) of the Highways Act 1980. The best way to avoid uncertainty is to use these procedures. They work in the interests of all parties, in particular by helping greatly to speed up the process of making definitive maps complete and accurate.

Depositing a map, statement and declaration does not take away any rights which have **already** been established through past use. However, depositing the documents will immediately fix a point at which any unacknowledged rights are brought into question. The onus will then be on anyone claiming that a right of way exists to demonstrate that it has already been established. Under deemed statutory dedication the 20-year period would thus be counted back from the date of the declaration. If any subsequent claims succeed, the deposited documents should be revised.

Reclassifying roads used as public paths

As there is confusion over exactly what rights the public have over ways shown on definitive maps as roads used as public paths (RUPPs), Section 54 of the Wildlife and Countryside Act 1981 requires highway authorities to make definitive map reclassification orders to reclassify each road used as a public path as:

- a byway open to all traffic if the public can be shown to have a right of way for vehicles; or
- a bridleway if no rights for vehicles can be shown to exist and bridleway rights have not been shown not to exist; or
- a footpath only if neither of the other options applies.

The procedure for reclassification orders is similar to that for modification orders. Again, it is concerned solely with recording the rights that already exist (and can therefore already be exercised). Highway authorities have to consider each road used as a public path in turn, examining the evidence, including evidence of historical rights, before deciding how to reclassify it. The condition of the way and its suitability, or otherwise, for motor traffic are not relevant factors and the authority is unable to take them into account. Reclassification as a byway open to all traffic does not place the authority under any obligation to surface the way specifically to make it suitable for motor vehicles.

Where there is concern about reclassification to a byway open to all traffic, the best course of action is to monitor usage by vehicles and to keep a detailed record of any damage caused. The level of use is unlikely to change following reclassification. However, if problems arise then sound evidence will assist the highway authority in encouraging voluntary restraint by user groups, self-policing by user groups, or other management measures, including, if appropriate, Traffic Regulation Orders (see also pages 62–63).

> **Key points: Resolving uncertainty**
>
> - Check the paths on the ground against the definitive map and statement and ask for advice from the authority if paths appear to be wrongly recorded.
>
> - The map and statement can be changed only by a definitive map modification order made by the highway authority.
>
> - Follow the set procedures when applying to alter the map. Most highway authorities can provide information on how to prepare applications. You should discuss the evidence with the highway authority beforehand.
>
> - Anyone can apply to have the map amended but they must have evidence to support the change. The evidence can be based on use or drawn from a range of documentary sources.
>
> - There is no point in seeking to oppose reclassification of a road used as a public path as a byway open to all traffic where vehicular rights are known to exist. This will simply waste the time and resources of all concerned.
>
> - See pages 72–74 for sources of further information.

Maintenance and protection

Responsibility for keeping public rights of way open is shared by highway authorities and the occupiers of land. Broadly, highway authorities have a duty to maintain the surface of public rights of way, and occupiers to keep them free of obstructions. When those responsibilities are not honoured, highway authorities, landowners, occupiers and users can all take action. Non-metropolitan district councils, parish or town councils and voluntary groups may also have a role in looking after public rights of way.

Duties and responsibilities

Highway authorities are currently the county, metropolitan district or outer London borough councils. Some non-metropolitan district councils and national park authorities act as agents for their county council, but the ultimate responsibility remains with the county council. Within any council, responsibility for rights of way work may rest with several departments.

The highway authority, specifically the rights of way officer, or department, should always be first point of contact for landowners and occupiers. This should be the quickest way of contacting someone who can assist and take appropriate action. Some authorities now publish information sheets setting out the services and standards offered by each department.

Parish and town councils, or parish meetings also have certain discretionary powers. They can: maintain any public footpath or bridleway in the parish; require the highway authority to secure the removal of an obstruction; erect signposts and waymarks with the consent of the highway authority; and insist that the highway authority carries out its duty to signpost and waymark rights of way where they leave metalled roads.

Most public rights of way are 'maintainable at public expense'. It is for the highway authority to maintain the surface so that it is suitable for the expected use.

Occupiers are under a duty not to obstruct any public right of way. They must allow any member of the public to use a right of way, according to its status, at any time. On tenanted land, the responsibilities of the occupier fall on the tenant, not the landlord. Elsewhere, it is the owner-occupier who is responsible. 'Obstruction' has been interpreted by the courts to cover anything which could inconvenience or endanger the public in any way or discourage use.

Highway authorities should:

- maintain the surface of highways, and control vegetation (other than crops) on the surface of field-edge paths and those enclosed by hedges, fences or walls and on set-aside land;

- maintain bridges over natural water courses including farm ditches (if the ditch was there when the path was first recorded);

- provide signposts where rights of way leave metalled roads (highway authorities may also waymark rights of way, after consulting the landowner);

- assert and protect the public's rights to use public rights of way;

- secure the removal of obstructions including those due to damage to the surface;

- ensure that there are no intimidating notices that deter the public from using paths shown on the definitive map, and prosecute anyone who displays such notices;

- take action, in default where necessary, to ensure that the duties of others are carried out;

- provide a minimum 25 per cent contribution towards any costs incurred by a landowner in maintaining stiles or gates on public rights of way.

Occupiers should:

- keep rights of way clear of any obstructions, such as padlocked gates, rubbish, barbed wire, slurry, manure, electric fences, hedgerows and chained or loose dogs, and warn users of potential dangers (eg slurry lagoons, cliffs) near rights of way;

- cut back vegetation encroaching from the sides (but not the surface), and above, so that it does not inconvenience the public or prevent the line of the right of way being apparent on the ground. (On bridleways, horse-riders should be allowed 3 metres (10 feet) of headroom);

- keep paths clear of crops (other than hay and silage) to ensure that they do not inconvenience users;

- ensure that stiles and gates on rights of way are maintained in good order: a minimum contribution of 25 per cent of the cost of any works may be claimed by the occupier from the highway authority (some authorities provide materials, for example stile kits, and others may carry out the work themselves);
- provide adequate bridges where, with the permission of the highway authority, new ditches are made or existing ones widened;
- ensure that cross-field footpaths and bridleways are cultivated (ie ploughed or disturbed) **only** when it is not convenient to avoid them;
- ensure that field-edge footpaths and bridleways and all byways open to all traffic, roads used as public paths and unsurfaced public roads are **never** cultivated;
- where the cultivation of a cross-field footpath or bridleway cannot be conveniently avoided, ensure that its surface is made good to at least the minimum width, so that it is reasonably convenient to use, within 14 days of first being cultivated for that crop, or within 24 hours of any subsequent cultivation (unless a longer period has been agreed in advance in writing by the highway authority);
- ensure that paths over cultivated land remain apparent on the ground, to at least the minimum width, at all times and are not obstructed by growing crops;
- ensure that bulls are not kept in a field crossed by a path unless they do not exceed 10 months old or are both not of a recognised dairy breed and are accompanied by cows or heifers (see also page 70);
- ensure that any warning notices are displayed **only** when a bull is present in a field;
- never keep an animal known to be aggressive (including any bull of whatever breed) in a field to which the public has any access;
- waymark rights of way (where occupiers consider it necessary and desirable);
- ensure that no misleading signs are placed near rights of way that might discourage access: highway authorities have powers under Section 57 of the National Parks and Access to the Countryside Act 1949 to remove such signs.

Practical action

The basic duties placed on highway authorities and occupiers should be observed in relation to all public rights of way and public roads. This does not mean that there is no flexibility. For example, the timing of action to restore cultivated paths can be varied, provided that prior written permission has been given by the highway authority. Similarly, a new fence may be erected across a footpath provided that prior written permission has been obtained to provide a gate or stile.

Where there is any doubt over maintenance responsibilities, or over the implications of any land management changes for public rights of way, appropriate advice and, if necessary, permission should always be sought beforehand from the highway authority.

A common source of confusion is the width of a public right of way. Where the definitive statement gives a width for a public right of way, then that is the minimum which must be respected. It is not uncommon for paths set out under the Inclosure Acts to be up to 18 metres (60 feet) wide. Where no width is given, then the following widths apply in relation to ploughing and cultivation:

- where a cross-field footpath is cultivated, it must be restored to a minimum width of 1 metre;
- where a cross-field bridleway is cultivated, it must be restored to a minimum width of 2 metres;
- other cross-field highways must not be cultivated: a minimum width of 3 metres must be respected;
- a field-edge footpath must not be cultivated: a minimum width of 1.5 metres must be respected;
- a field-edge bridleway must not be cultivated: a minimum width of 3 metres must be respected;
- other field-edge highways must not be cultivated: a minimum width of 5 metres must be respected.

These widths do not affect other aspects of the law on public paths and do not limit established public rights of passage.

Enforcement

Highway authorities are under a duty to protect and assert public rights of way. In dealing with owners and occupiers they are not bound to make approaches initially by letter, or in person, but they often do so. The highway authority may serve a notice on an occupier requiring an obstruction to be removed, or may post a notice on the land if the person cannot be identified. If no action is taken within the specified period, the authority may enter the land, carry out the works it thinks are necessary and recover the costs from the occupier. Alternatively, or in addition, the authority may prosecute the occupier in a magistrates' court.

The power to prosecute an occupier for failing to keep a cross-field or field-edge right of way clear of growing crops is also available to any individual person. Where highway authorities take action to restore cross-field or field-edge rights of way, or to clear them of growing crops or other obstructions, they may work to the following maximum widths (unless a narrower width is set out in the definitive statement): 1.8 metres for any footpath; 3 metres for any bridleway; and 5 metres for any other unsurfaced public highway.

Where cultivations are carried out by a contractor, rather than the occupier, it is the occupier who will be held liable for any failure to restore cross-field footpaths or bridleways, or to avoid any other cross-field right of way, or any field-edge right of way. This underlines the importance of all those involved in day-to-day land management being aware of the rights of way shown on the definitive map and statement.

If the highway authority fails to carry out its maintenance duties, Section 56 of the Highways Act 1980 provides for any person affected to serve notice on the authority to repair the highway. It is important in these circumstances to establish what has caused the problem. The highway authority need only maintain a right of way so that it is suitable for the ordinary traffic of the neighbourhood. Where damage can be attributed to use of a right of way by farm vehicles, the authority may ask the owner or occupier to help defray the costs involved.

The division of responsibility between highway authorities and occupiers over the clearance of paths on set-aside land has been a further source of confusion. Advice from MAFF can be summarised as follows:

- Land which is set-aside under the Arable Area Payments Scheme or the Five Year Set-Aside Scheme is still considered to be in agricultural use. It follows that the provisions of the Highways Act 1980 relating to ploughing and cultivation still apply to that land. Similarly, rights of way across set-aside land should be kept clear of game cover or non-food crops.

- Where the necessary vegetation cover is provided by allowing natural regeneration, the resultant growth may or may not obstruct the right of way concerned. Where the cover consists predominantly of volunteers from the previous crop, it may be considered to be a crop and responsibility for clearing it will rest with the occupier. Where the cover consists predominantly of grasses and other plants not sown by the occupier, responsibility for clearing it will rest with the highway authority.

- Where it appears that a right of way on set-aside land is, or is likely to become, blocked by naturally regenerated growth, the occupier should contact the highway authority as soon as possible to discuss how it may best be dealt with. Any action by the highway authority will not absolve the occupier from the responsibility to manage the set-aside land and, where appropriate, cut the cover in accordance with the set-aside management rules. When doing so, regard should always be had to rights of way.

Payment schemes and voluntary assistance

Some authorities enter into voluntary maintenance agreements with farmers and landowners. Under these, in return for modest payments, farmers agree to mow (or otherwise control) vegetation on the surface of a path which is the highway authority's responsibility. They may do this on their own land alone, or over several farms. Such agreements are increasingly used for headland paths. They can benefit all interests.

Parish councils are increasingly being encouraged to participate in schemes to survey, restore and maintain their local network of public rights of way. The 'Parish Paths Partnership' which operates through some highway authorities, encourages local people to become involved in keeping their paths in good order.

Other examples of collaborative projects include 'Adopt-a-Path' schemes, and projects run by Groundwork Trusts. Path user groups and Young Farmers' Clubs are often keen to get involved in work which helps to keep rights of way open and usable. Landowners and farmers may well find it worthwhile to contact those running local initiatives.

Key points: Maintenance and protection

- Be aware of your responsibilities, as occupier, for public rights of way and roads on your land.

- Be aware of the responsibilities of the highway authority for maintaining public rights of way; find out who manages its work in your area.

- Take appropriate action where you or your employees discover any problems which it is your responsibility to solve; find out what help may be available from the highway authority or other local authority.

- Tell the highway authority of any problems which are their responsibility; make sure the authority carries out all its duties.

- Find out whether the highway authority operates any maintenance agreements with farmers and landowners.

- Keep in touch with your town or parish council; find out if it is involved in the Parish Paths Partnership.

- Ask local volunteer groups, eg from the Ramblers' Association, British Horse Society, Young Farmers' Clubs or British Trust for Conservation Volunteers, to help with path clearance projects.
- If you are concerned about any works to rights of way on your land, contact the highway authority immediately.
- See pages 72–74 for sources of further information.

Improving the network

Viewed on a map, the network of public rights of way and other minor highways may appear illogical and anachronistic. The temptation for a landowner or farmer to suggest a more 'rational' network can be strong. Some may feel that there are just too many paths, or that many are never used and could be closed. Others may believe that although the paths over their land historically made sense, they now threaten the security of the farm holding, conflict with modern farming methods or do not meet modern recreational needs. Local residents and path users may similarly wish to see changes in the network to give access to new areas or increase their enjoyment of the countryside.

Rights of way and other highways **can** be changed, but **only** for the reasons specified in legislation, and **only** through prescribed, statutory procedures. This section outlines what is involved in making such changes, and how the procedures can be used to best effect.

Mark Boulton/CC

Changes to footpaths and bridleways

Most changes to footpaths and bridleways come about through public path orders made under the Highways Act 1980. Highway authorities and non-metropolitan district councils may all make such orders to create, extinguish (stop-up or close) or divert paths.

Orders to divert or extinguish paths can also be made under the Town and Country Planning Act 1990 to enable development to take place. 'Development' includes buildings or works for which planning permission has been granted (eg the construction of golf courses) and those that are 'permitted development', for which specific planning permission is not required (eg many new agricultural buildings). In such cases it is the planning authority for the area that makes the order. The words "to enable development" are important; this type of order cannot be made or confirmed once the development is completed, or is substantially complete. Some other way will have to be found of resolving the problem (which might include demolishing the building).

The procedures for diverting or extinguishing a path to enable development to take place are quite separate from the granting of planning permission. If a development site is crossed by a right of way and a change is desired, then the onus is on the owner or developer to seek the appropriate order. The change is not made automatically as a consequence of the grant of planning permission. Nor is the order necessarily assured of success. Such orders can be opposed, and may consequently not be confirmed.

Because public rights are affected, the process of deciding whether and how paths should change is also a public one in which anyone is entitled to express their view and have it taken into account. The general principles are:

(a) Anyone can apply to the highway authority or non-metropolitan district council for the area to make a public path order. The power to make an order is entirely discretionary: the authority cannot be compelled to do so, nor is there any right of appeal against a refusal.

(b) An applicant who expects to gain some financial or other benefit, whether directly or indirectly, from extinguishing or diverting a path, will normally be expected to bear at least part of the costs associated with the order.

(c) Before deciding whether to make a path order, most authorities carry out wide consultations with all the owners and occupiers of the affected land, the parish council and any other local authority for the area, and path user groups. (Depending on the type of order, some or all of these consultations may also be a statutory requirement).

(d) Before making an order, the authority must be satisfied that the proposal meets the tests and criteria laid down in the legislation relevant to the type of order.

(e) Making an order is only the start of the formal process. The proposals will then be publicised (by advertisement in a local newspaper and a notice and plan put up on the path), and a copy of the order will be served on the owners and occupiers of the land, the parish council and various other bodies and organisations that might be affected by it.

(f) If no objections are received within 28 days, or any received are withdrawn, the authority may then confirm the order itself (providing it does not change it in any way).

(g) If objections are received (or if the authority wishes to change the order), a decision on whether or not to confirm the order will be made not by the authority but by an Inspector appointed by the Secretary of State for the Environment.

(h) If there are only two or three objections, the matter will normally be dealt with by an exchange of correspondence (the 'written representations' procedure). Otherwise a public inquiry will be arranged to hear the arguments for and against the proposals. The Inspector will also visit the site.

(i) If and when the order is confirmed (either by the authority or the Inspector) further notices will be issued and the decision will be publicised.

(j) Depending on the type of order and how it is worded, the changes will either legally take effect when the order is confirmed (or a set number of days after that date), or will not take effect until the highway authority is satisfied that the new path is ready for use.

A more detailed explanation is given in *A guide to procedures for public path orders* (CCP 449), published by the Countryside Commission.

These procedures are designed to balance the respective public and private interests in rights of way and the land which they cross. Although they may appear to be long and daunting, the great majority of path orders made each year are unopposed. It is not true that "the Ramblers will object to everything" (statistically, objections are more likely to come from a neighbour or other local people). However, to try to change a path when it or the adjoining paths cannot be used easily, or when public rights of passage are not otherwise being respected, invites opposition. Nor are proposals which disregard the interests of the public or the owner and occupier likely to succeed. Extensive reorganisation proposals may arouse particular concern: it is better to deal with paths one at a time. The key lies in careful preparation to ensure that any proposals that are made are as fair and balanced as possible.

A landowner or farmer who wishes to change the path network should start by discussing the problem that has given rise to the need for the change with the highway authority. Advice should be sought on the policies of the highway authority and any district council on changing the network, and on what other solutions might be possible. Problems of unintentional trespass, for example, can often be solved by ensuring the line of the path is clear on the ground and well waymarked. Help may be available to deal with a recurring maintenance problem, or it may be possible to organise farming practices to fit in better with the path network, rather than the other way round. Such solutions, if they can be found, will nearly always be preferable to diverting or closing a public right of way.

Widespread informal consultations prior to making a public path order are essential. Authorities vary in the approach they take; some encourage (or expect) the applicant to take the lead and will give advice about who should be approached and the kind of concerns that are likely to be raised. Others prefer to take the lead themselves. The aim should be to identify as many as possible of the interests that people have in the path network, and develop proposals that not only satisfy the relevant legal tests but are accepted by everyone as being both necessary and fair. This will often mean considering alternative ideas, and might mean abandoning proposals if it is clear that they will be strongly opposed. The 'do nothing' option should always be evaluated alongside other proposals for change.

Before making a formal request to change the network, landowners or farmers should consider all of the following questions:

- Have I identified precisely the problem that the changes are designed to solve?

- Am I certain that the changes being proposed will deal with the problem; that this is the only practical way of doing so; and that the changes will not themselves give rise to further problems?

- What will be the benefits to me in land management terms?

- What effect will my proposals have on other people's use and enjoyment, both of the paths on my land and the wider path network in the area?

- Have I spoken to local people and to the appropriate path user groups to find out what they think? What advantages will they gain?

- Are my proposals likely to satisfy the legal tests that the authority has to apply? In particular, will a proposal to extinguish a path satisfy the test that the path 'is not needed for public use'? If not, then a diversion proposal might stand a greater chance of success.

- Am I certain that the proposals do not go against the authority's own interests in any way, eg by adding to their maintenance liabilities?

- Are all the existing paths that are affected by the proposals open and available for use, as the law requires they should be?
- Have I demonstrated my willingness to respect public rights by honouring my responsibilities for all rights of way on my land?
- Have I taken any other advice that may be available, eg from the CLA or NFU?
- Can I still modify my proposals, if necessary, to meet any further concerns that are raised?

It would, however, be unrealistic to expect that informal agreement can always be reached in every case. Genuine differences will sometimes remain which can only be properly resolved at a local inquiry, at which all the interests can air their views and a fair decision can be reached reflecting the overall balance of opinion. Nor can informal consultations necessarily identify all the points of view or issues. New ones may sometimes arise only after an order has been made and advertised, when everyone who may use the path becomes aware of the proposals.

Grounds for making an order and the tests to be satisfied:

1. Footpath and bridleway orders (Highways Act, 1980):

Section 26: Creating a new path

- It must appear to the authority that there is a need for the new path and they must be satisfied that it is expedient to create it having regard to :
   - the extent to which it would add to the convenience or enjoyment of a substantial section of the public or of local residents;
   - the effect which the creation would have on the rights of those with an interest in the land, taking into account the provisions for compensation.

Section 118: Extinguishing a path

- Before making an order, it must appear to the authority that it is expedient to extinguish (stop-up or close) the path on the ground that it is not needed for public use.
- Before confirming an order the authority or the Secretary of State must be satisfied that it is expedient to confirm it having regard to the extent to which the path is likely to be used and the effect which closure would have on land served by it, taking into account the provisions for compensation.

- Both in making and confirming an order, the authority and the Secretary of State must disregard any temporary circumstances preventing or diminishing the use of the path by the public.

Section 119: Diverting a path

- Before making an order the authority must be satisfied that it is expedient to divert the path in the interests either of the public or of the owner, lessee or occupier of the land crossed by the path.

- The authority must also be satisfied that the diversion order does not alter any point of termination of the path, other than to another point on the same path, or another highway connected with it, and which is substantially as convenient to the public. The point of termination cannot be altered where this is not on a highway (ie a cul-de-sac).

- Before confirming an order the authority or the Secretary of State must be satisfied that:
  - the diversion is expedient in the interests of the person(s) stated in the order;
  - the path will not be substantially less convenient to the public as a consequence of the diversion;
  - it is expedient to confirm the order having regard to the effect it will have on public enjoyment of the path as a whole, on other land served by the existing path and on land affected by any proposed new path, taking into account the provisions for compensation.

2. Orders to enable development to take place (Town and Country Planning Act, 1990):

Section 257: Diverting or extinguishing paths

- Before making an order the authority must be satisfied that it is necessary to do so to enable development to be carried out:
  - in accordance with a planning permission that has been granted;
  - that is 'permitted development' under a General or Special Development Order;
  - by a Government department.

- Before confirming an opposed order the Secretary of State must also be satisfied that the above criteria have been met.

The costs of path orders

The Local Authorities (Recovery of Costs of Public Path Orders) Regulations 1993 enable authorities to recover from the applicant their costs associated with any of the diversion or extinguishment orders described above, or for a creation order made concurrently with an extinguishment order. The costs that may be recovered include administrative costs up to a maximum of £400 for an order relating to one path, plus £75 for each additional path. This limit is to be reviewed in 1995. The applicant will also be expected to bear the costs of advertising the order in one local newspaper. Three such advertisements may be needed: on the making, confirmation and coming into effect of the order.

The authority has discretion, however, to take into account factors such as the applicant's financial hardship or the potential benefits to the public of the changes proposed. All or part of the charge may be waived where appropriate. The fact that an order is not confirmed does not mean that the applicant is automatically entitled to a refund, but costs will normally be refunded if the authority decides not to proceed (eg if it fails to confirm an unopposed order) or if the order cannot be confirmed because it has been invalidly made.

Applicants for orders can also be required to meet the costs of any physical works needed to construct a new path and any compensation that may be payable arising from a diversion order under Section 119 of the 1980 Act (eg where the diversion puts the path onto a neighbour's land).

It is Government policy that the parties at a public inquiry are expected to meet their own expenses irrespective of the outcome. Costs against any party will be awarded only exceptionally, eg if they are shown to have behaved unreasonably. Costs will, however, normally be awarded to any person with an interest in land affected by a path creation order who successfully objects to it.

Changes to byways and other highways

The procedures outlined above apply only to footpaths and bridleways. Orders to divert or extinguish byways open to all traffic, or other minor highways with vehicular rights, are normally made under Section 116 of the Highways Act 1980 and follow substantially different procedures. Such orders are made not by the highway authority, but by the magistrates' court (on the application of the highway authority) and it is the magistrates who also determine any objections. The parish council can veto an order by refusing to consent to the authority's application. Anyone who requests the highway authority to make an application may be asked to meet the whole of the authority's costs.

It is occasionally necessary to use these powers in connection with a footpath or bridleway, for example where it is being dealt with at the same time as a vehicular right of way. However, the Secretary of State for the Environment has advised authorities that they should not use these powers in respect of footpaths and bridleways unless there are good reasons for doing so.

Geoff King/NFU

'Unofficial' and temporary diversions

The only course of action that is open to anyone who wants to change a right of way is to try to persuade the highway authority or non-metropolitan district council for the area to make the necessary order. Anyone who 'unofficially' closes or alters the line of a path, even temporarily, runs the risk of being prosecuted by the highway authority and of having to pay the authority's costs in removing the obstruction. In addition, path users are not obliged to follow the unofficial line, but if they do there is a possibility, over time, that a second public right of way might be created by deemed dedication.

The highway authority may make an order to divert a footpath or bridleway temporarily for up to three months, in connection with any excavation or engineering operation that is reasonably necessary for agricultural purposes. There is no requirement for the order to be advertised or any opportunity for objections to be made; a notice and plan showing the alternative route are simply displayed at either end of the diversion while it is in force.

Rights of way can also be temporarily closed or diverted for up to six months through a Traffic Regulation Order made by the highway authority but only to enable works to be carried out on or near the road or because of the likelihood of danger to the public. Section 261 of the Town and Country Planning Act 1990 also provides for temporary closures to enable mineral extraction. Section 23 of the Animal Health Act 1981 enables the Minister of Agriculture, Fisheries and Food to prohibit entry to a notified area 'infected' by certain animal diseases such as foot and mouth disease. Such an order has the effect of prohibiting the use of rights of way across the land.

Creation of new rights of way by express dedication or agreement

New paths or ways can be beneficial for many different reasons. They could encourage people away from problem areas by providing an interesting or exciting alternative, perhaps along an escarpment or to a viewpoint. They could form a missing link in a circular walk from a village, thus enabling local people to enjoy the countryside on their doorstep. They could provide the answer to continued trespass over a myriad of different routes through crops or to disturbance of stock or game which happens because people want to visit a particular place but there is no defined path for them to use.

There are three ways in which new rights of way can be created other than by a creation order (see pages 37–42) or by deemed dedication under statute or common law (see pages 14 and 15). These are: express dedication by the landowner; creation by agreement with the highway authority or non-metropolitan district council; and creation by agreement with the parish or town council. Only the freehold owner of the land has the legal capacity to dedicate a right of way.

Express dedication occurs where landowners consciously and deliberately give the public the right to use a way over their land. Certain conditions must be satisfied: it must be intended to dedicate the way as a public right of way; the public must actually use the way (ie it must be accepted by the public); it must be for the public at large, not merely for local people or some other group; and it must not be for a specified period only. The path that is created will not be maintainable at public expense.

County and district councils have the power to enter into creation agreements under Section 25 of the Highways Act 1980. Such agreements between the landowner and the authority, can incorporate any agreed conditions, set out specific maintenance responsibilities and provide for payment. Some authorities have standard schemes for this purpose. Parish and town councils can also enter into agreements to create rights of way under Section 30 of the 1980 Act. However, there is no provision for payment in such cases or for paths created in this way to be maintainable at public expense.

Ian Allen/CC

Key points: Improving the network

- Changes to rights of way and other highways can only be made for one or other of the reasons specified in legislation, and can only come about by following prescribed, statutory procedures.

- Highway authorities and non-metropolitan district councils have discretionary powers to make orders to create, extinguish or divert footpaths and bridleways; but they cannot be compelled to make orders.

- Making an order is the start of the formal process. The order is then advertised and anyone may object to it.

- Proposals which do not carefully balance public and private interests, or are not widely accepted as being both necessary and fair, are unlikely to succeed.

- If you are considering asking for changes to be made to the paths on your land, take early advice from the highway authority and consider what other solutions to the problem might be possible.

- Develop any proposals for change in wide consultation with all the interests likely to be affected: be prepared to modify your proposals.

- Always consider the 'do nothing' option alongside other possibilities: be prepared to abandon your proposals.

- If you expect to gain financially from any changes, you will normally be required to contribute to the authority's costs in making a path order and to bear other substantial expenses associated with it.

- You can also create new paths by dedication or by agreement: doing so could be beneficial for many reasons, both to the public and to you.

- Do not 'unofficially' close or divert a public path: this is illegal and action could be taken against you.

- See pages 72–74 for sources of further information.

4. PROVIDING ACCESS BY AGREEMENT

There are many opportunities for landowners and farmers to provide access by agreement to land not already subject to a legal right of access. Providing additional access can have several important advantages:

- providing managed access in one part of a farm or estate can help reduce problems of trespass elsewhere;
- providing managed access is increasingly encouraged under Government schemes and can provide useful supplementary income;
- providing new access opportunities can help build goodwill towards farmers and landowners from the local community and visitors.

Any new provision for access should be developed as a partnership between farmers and landowners and user groups (eg with a sports club), local authorities (eg over permitted paths), statutory agencies (eg under the Countryside Stewardship scheme) or the Ministry of Agriculture, Fisheries and Food (eg under the Countryside Access Scheme). Such partnerships can not only deliver financial benefits to landowners and farmers but also assistance in managing access and solving problems. For example, sports clubs can often be relied upon to ensure that their members behave properly.

Several Government and statutory agency schemes are now available to encourage provision for both informal and formal recreation. Many local authorities can also offer assistance although they have no statutory duty to do so. Where public money is involved, the access secured will be publicised. However, providing access by permission or agreement confers no long term rights. Use can be time-limited and with conditions, thus allowing a greater degree of management flexibility.

The opportunities for farmers and landowners include: additional 'permitted' routes for use by the general public or specific groups (see pages 47–49); areas where people can walk, cycle or ride freely, with permission (see pages 49–54); sites for individual sports or events, with permission (see pages 54–57); or provision for those with special needs (see pages 57 and 58).

New routes

New routes for public use can be created by dedicating a public right of way (see pages 44 and 45) or by establishing permitted (or 'permissive') paths or toll-rides (see pages 48 and 49). New routes or areas for public access can also be provided under Government schemes (see pages 49–54).

Permitted paths

A permitted path is not a public right of way but a route which can be used by the public with the permission of the landowner. The duty of care to users of permitted paths lies with the landowner (see pages 10–12). So too does responsibility for maintaining permitted paths. On publicly-maintainable rights of way these responsibilities lie with the highway authority. Permitted paths should be seen as a supplement to the rights of way network, not as a substitute for rights of way.

Permitted paths should always be the subject of formal agreements between landowners and highway authorities, so that there is no possibility of confusion at any later date over the status of the path. Conditions may be included, for example restricting use to daylight hours only, that dogs must be kept on a lead, or that the path may be closed at certain times of the year. Notices to this effect should be posted at either end of a permitted path.

Entering into a formal agreement should in particular help to avoid any possibility of a subsequent claim being made that it was intended to dedicate a permitted path as a right of way. Model forms of permitted path agreement are available from the CLA (see pages 72–74). It is helpful to reinforce them with a map, statement and statutory declaration made under Section 31(6) of the Highways Act 1980 (see pages 24–27).

Toll-rides

An alternative to an agreement with a highway authority is an agreement with a specific group of users. For example many horse riders are keen to get their horses off busy, main roads or dangerous, narrow lanes. They may be willing to pay an annual fee to use safe and quiet 'toll-rides' which link with public bridleways, byways open to all traffic, or unsurfaced public roads.

Various toll-ride organisations now exist in parts of England to negotiate the provision of toll-rides on behalf of scattered groups of riders. Toll-ride systems are operating well in several areas. They provide a network of short links between existing routes, or longer circular rides with more than one access point to the circuit. In some areas jumps or exercise fields have also been provided.

Riders who participate in a toll-ride scheme pay an annual licence toll. Such schemes usually require users to wear coloured armbands issued to them and to observe certain safety rules. Horse-riding groups are often keen to administer such schemes and to co-ordinate links over land in different ownership. Toll-rides should never be confused with public bridleways: they should be seen as additions to the network. Nor should they be routed along public footpaths. In some cases it can be much better for all interests to establish new bridleway links by agreement with the highway authority rather than toll-rides.

> ### Key points: New routes
>
> - Examine the network of paths crossing your property and also your neighbours' land.
>
> - Consider the scope for providing permitted paths by agreement with the highway authority to supplement rights of way and create circular walks or rides.
>
> - Take professional advice before signing any agreement, especially if operating a licence scheme with specific groups.
>
> - See pages 72–74 for sources of further information.
>
> - See pages 75–77 for the addresses of toll-ride organisations in the South East, East Anglia, Avon (Old Down) and Derbyshire (Amber Valley).

Access to areas of land

There are various schemes under which landowners and farmers can provide public access to areas of land in return for payments. These are operated by Government departments, statutory agencies and local authorities. Informal arrangements can also be made, without payment.

Access agreements may specify restrictions on public use, eg access must be on foot only, entry must be via certain access points, dogs must be kept on leads, or camping is not permitted. Access may be suspended temporarily, eg to reduce the risk of fire during very dry weather, or to prevent the spread of a livestock disease. Byelaws may also be made as an additional control over public behaviour.

In return, access agreements may place certain obligations on the owner, eg to notify the relevant authority before carrying-out certain types of work on the agreement land or to farm the land following a specified management regime. Access agreements will usually be publicised on site through notices at access points or nearby parking areas, and sometimes on maps available to the public.

Ministry of Agriculture schemes

Two schemes have been announced by the Ministry of Agriculture, Fisheries and Food: the Countryside Access Scheme, applicable to non-rotational set-aside land; and the Access Tier, applicable to land under agreements in Environmentally Sensitive Areas.

The Countryside Access Scheme is expected to open to applicants in autumn 1994. It is a voluntary scheme open to farmers who have land in non-rotational set-aside under the Arable Area Payments Scheme. Its objective is to provide new opportunities for public access to suitable set-aside land for walking and other forms of quiet recreation.

The scheme targets only land which is particularly suited for new or increased public access (eg land providing access to a vantage point or attractive landscape feature linking two or more existing access ways). Farmers entering land into the scheme are required to manage the land in accordance with the set-aside rules, and also to observe a range of other conditions including maintaining free passage over the land, providing and maintaining adequate means of entry, and keeping the land free of litter and other refuse. The access opportunities will be publicised.

The annual management payments to farmers are based on 10-metre wide access strips along field margins and/or on whole or part fields. The payments reflect the costs incurred, and have been set during 1994/5 at £90 per hectare for access strips (ie £90 per kilometre) and £45 per hectare for whole or part fields.

The Access Tier is a voluntary management option already open to applications from farmers managing land under agreements in Environmentally Sensitive Areas (ESAs). The Tier operates in all 22 English ESAs and its objective is to provide new opportunities for public access for walking and other quiet recreation in parts of the countryside which have been designated as being of particular environmental importance.

The Tier is targeted on land which is particularly suitable for new or significantly increased access (eg land providing access to a vantage point or linking two or more existing access ways). Land accepted into the Tier remains subject to the environmental management conditions of the ESA in question and farmers also have to maintain free passage over the land, provide and maintain adequate means of entry, keep the land free of litter and other refuse and respect other conditions designed to ensure that access can be enjoyed by the public without imperilling environmental objectives. The access opportunities will be publicised.

The annual management payments made to farmers are based on 10-metre wide access strips along the sides of or across fields. The payments reflect the costs incurred and have been set at £170 per kilometre (£274 per mile). 80 per cent grants are available on capital investments (eg stiles and footbridges) required as a result of participation in the Tier. Signboards and waymarks are provided free of charge.

Countryside Stewardship

Countryside Stewardship is a pilot scheme operated by the Countryside Commission on behalf of the Department of the Environment and in partnership with English Nature, English Heritage and the Ministry of Agriculture, Fisheries and Food. It is designed to protect, maintain, enhance or recreate certain traditional English landscapes (eg chalk downland, heathland, enclosed moorland, coastal land, water meadows, historic landscapes and parklands).

The targeting arrangements favour land which is already used by the public, or to which the applicant is prepared to allow new access in return for an additional premium. This may take a number of forms;

- new areas of open access, for example attractive picnic sites or small areas for informal recreation close to villages and towns;
- new permissive linear paths, such as footpaths or bridleways to open up viewpoints and provide new circular routes or links to the existing public rights of way network;
- new opportunities for using land for educational visits, especially sites that are readily accessible and that offer some special interest.

Payments may also be made for the provision of management services which improve access, eg maintaining new paths through long grass or scrub or providing new or improved opportunities for people with disabilities or mobility problems to enjoy the countryside.

Payments for access are not available in respect of public rights of way or other rights of access or where there is an established tradition of access (ie *de facto* access). Access under the scheme is permissive and no new rights of way will be created (although there is scope to agree new rights under special arrangements). Agreements under the scheme last for 10 years. The payments currently available in 1994 are:

- £150   per year base payment for new access provision; and
  - £35 per hectare per year for open access in lowlands or in-bye land in upland areas; or
  - £0.15 per metre per year for permissive footpaths, or £0.30 per metre per year for permissive bridleways or paths for disabled people;
- £400   per year for land made available for educational visits.

Capital payments are also available for features such as new gates, stiles and footbridges provided in connection with the new access. Where there is potential to provide safe access for the disabled, or those with a mobility problem, capital payments are available to help with laying suitable paths.

Basic conditions applying to the access option under Countryside Stewardship

Access will be publicised by the Countryside Commission to ensure people know the land is available, and to encourage use suited to the size and nature of the site. A county register of access land will be compiled. Agreement holders will be required to notify their local parish councils about the availability of access.

Conditions include:

- Access to the agreed land must be available without charge to the public for quiet countryside enjoyment on foot and, where appropriate, for horse-riding and pedal-cycling.
- Areas and paths should be kept safe for users and free from litter. Stiles and gates should be kept in a good, usable condition.
- The land, paths and bridleways should be clearly marked by map boards and waymarked where appropriate.
- Dogs may be required to be kept on a lead when stock are present.
- Public rights of way over land must not be restricted or modified.
- Permissive paths should be a minimum width of 2 metres ($6^{1}/_{2}$ feet) for footpaths, and 3 metres (10 feet) for bridleways.
- A surface that is suitable for all agreed users should be maintained.
- Applicants are expected to ensure they have public liability insurance cover of at least £1 million.

To allow for field sports and pest control, the land and permissive paths may be closed to the public for up to 10 days in each year (but not on public holidays) provided prior notice is given. It must be made clear that the closure does not affect any public rights of way. The Countryside Commission may agree that land can be closed for longer periods for specific purposes.

Other schemes

The Forestry Authority offers a one-off Community Woodland Supplement of £950 per hectare for a 10-year period under its Woodland Grant Scheme to encourage new woodlands to be planted and made available for public access close to towns and cities. Existing woodlands where access is provided and new woodlands may also qualify for management grants of up to £35 per hectare per year. In special cases, discretionary capital payments may be made for significant environmental improvements.

English Heritage may provide grant aid to encourage the presentation of scheduled ancient monuments and important archaeological sites to the public, where public access is appropriate.

Local authority agreements

The largest areas with negotiated access arrangements are those areas of 'open country' covered by agreements under Section 64 of the National Parks and Access to the Countryside Act 1949. Such agreements provide for payments (which may, in practice, be nominal) and the application of byelaws and ranger services to the land involved.

'Open country' is defined, for the purposes of such agreements, as land consisting wholly or predominantly of: mountain, moor, heath and down; cliff and foreshore; woodland; rivers, canals, expanses of water through which rivers flow, and land adjacent to them.

Local authorities also have powers under Section 39 of the Wildlife and Countryside Act 1981 to enter into management agreements "for the purpose of conserving or enhancing the natural beauty or amenity of .... the countryside .... or promoting its enjoyment by the public". Such agreements have advantages in that they can apply to any type of rural land, not simply open country. They can also link public enjoyment with land management in a positive way.

Informal arrangements

Landowners are also at liberty to open any of their land to the public either on specific days in the year or for longer periods. Where agricultural land is concerned, it is important to check that doing so will not prejudice any claim for farm support payments. If no charge is being made for access (or if donations are invited for charity), then there should be no problem.

For many years, the National Gardens Scheme has encouraged private landowners to open their gardens for one or more days each year to raise funds for charities. A parallel scheme has recently been established by the Forestry Trust for Conservation and Education. The Trust also produces a guide to 'woodlands to visit'.

> **Key points: Access to areas of land**
> - Explore ways of improving access management on your land.
> - Weigh up the benefits and costs of entering one of the schemes to provide new public access or manage existing access.
> - Remember that the public expect value for money when access is financed with public funds.
> - See pages 72–74 for sources of further information.

Providing for formal activities

A whole range of popular sports require land, water or air to carry out their activities. Some of the demand for new facilities can be supplied by farmers making new use of both land and buildings. Many opportunities exist for farmers and landowners to get a reasonable financial return from satisfying the demand for appropriate sporting facilities.

Recently, the number of people taking part in both indoor and outdoor sports has grown. As a result, there is a growing demand for agreements between participants in sports and landowners to provide sites for recreational activities. Providing appropriate facilities in one part of a farm or estate may help to reduce problems of illegal use elsewhere.

Sports on farms can be profitable, but it is essential to consider all the possible implications for the farming business and way of life before making any commitments. All the implications of any arrangements should be investigated beforehand. Professional advice can be invaluable. Not all sports can be accommodated alongside existing traditional activities. The impact of the sport, both in the long and short term, needs careful consideration.

However, once a non-farming enterprise has been introduced on a farm, additional opportunities may present themselves. These could include the provision of: camping facilities, refreshments, the sale or hire of equipment, storage facilities, or on-farm accommodation.

Every farm is different, and resources need to be carefully assessed. These include land, labour, capital and other attributes, eg accessibility, remoteness and availability of public transport. Potential customers are another resource, and the judgement must be made whether sufficient local demand exists to make the project viable, or whether it will be dependent on a larger population catchment area.

> **Opportunities for providing facilities of recreational activities include the following:**
>
> - **Land-based:** adventure games, archery, clay-pigeon shooting, small-bore or pistol shooting, golf, cycling, motorsports (eg trail riding, off-road driving, autocycling), orienteering, skiing, tennis.
>
> - **Water-based:** angling, canoeing, diving, jet skis, dinghy sailing, water-skiing, wind-surfing, mooring and marina developments.
>
> - **Air-based:** hang-gliding, paragliding, model aeroplane flying, gliding, hot-air ballooning, microlighting, parachuting.
>
> - **Equestrian enterprises:** pony trekking, livery, cross-country courses, riding schools, toll-rides.
>
> - **Indoor sports (using existing buildings):** bowls, badminton, indoor cricket, squash.

The Ministry of Agriculture, Fisheries and Food has prepared four booklets on various farm diversification issues (see page 74 for further details).

Planning issues

Agriculture is largely exempt from planning control. But, if introducing a sports enterprise involves a material change in the use of a building or land, or the alternative use exceeds 28 days per year (14 in the case of competitive motorsports), planning permission will be necessary.

Structure Plans, Local Plans and Unitary Development Plans should set out local authority policies on recreational development in the countryside. Early consultation with the local planning authority is important.

When considering planning applications, the authority will take into account:
- national and local planning policies;
- effects on traffic, eg turning on and off public roads;
- effects on existing public rights of way (see also pages 37–42);
- impact of increased traffic on local residents and neighbouring farmers;
- disturbance, including noise, time of day when in use, pollution risks;
- the visual effects of the proposed development;
- views of nearby residents about the scheme;
- whether services (eg electricity, water, sewerage) are available.

Help in making planning applications should be available from the local planning authority. A planning consultant or land agent will prepare planning applications for a fee. The NFU or CLA can provide further advice. Detailed guidance for farmers and landowners on the planning system and on how to go about presenting proposals to the best effect is contained in *A Farmers Guide to the Planning System*, published jointly by the Ministry of Agriculture, Fisheries and Food, the Department of the Environment and the Welsh Office (see page 74).

Other matters

- **Insurance**: This should be checked at an early stage. Standard farming insurance policy is unlikely to provide adequate cover for public liability, construction work, etc.
- **Taxation**: Income should be declared and trading costs offset when determining the profit of the business. Professional advice should be sought on whether sports facilities can gain 'roll-over' relief, if the funds come from selling other assets. If a business is registered for VAT, and fees are charged, VAT should be deducted from the income.
- **Landlord's consent**: Most written tenancy agreements contain clauses which require a tenant to seek permission from the landlord before carrying out any non-agricultural activities on the holding. Any agreement should be checked, and any necessary written consent obtained beforehand.
- **Business rates**: Most forms of farm diversification will be liable for non-domestic rates even if the land is used for agriculture for part of the year. The local valuation office will be able to give further information.

> **Key points: Providing for formal activities**
>
> - Consider carefully the impact of any planned provision for sport on your own farming and other operations, and also the impact on the landscape and any existing public access.
>
> - Consult the local planning authority, your neighbours and local people.
>
> - Seek professional advice on planning and tax issues, legal liability, etc.
>
> - Ensure you understand the exact requirements of the sport: seek advice from the relevant governing body through the Central Council of Physical Recreation (see page 75).
>
> - Draw up a comprehensive business plan, including an objective projection of likely costs, time involvement, etc.
>
> - Carry out the necessary market research to identify likely demand/projected income.
>
> - Make sure the new activities or land users do not prejudice existing rights, either public or private, or contravene the terms or conditions of any management agreement or grant.
>
> - Think in terms of a 'leisure package' to attract greater numbers of visitors.
>
> - See pages 72–74 for sources of further information.

Access for those with special needs

Many opportunities to enjoy the countryside are effectively denied to anyone whose mobility is impaired, even if only slightly. Stiles, uneven or boggy paths and other common features of the countryside can present impenetrable barriers to the elderly, people in wheelchairs and others with special needs. Many local authorities are now endeavouring to address these needs, however, by adapting and promoting suitable rights of way and by providing other facilities and features. Landowners are encouraged to cooperate, for example in helping to select suitable routes or by allowing the authority to replace standard stiles with self-closing gates that can be used by people in wheelchairs.

Simply ensuring that popular paths are easy to use by replacing stiles with kissing gates and removing other unintentional barriers can increase enormously the accessibility and enjoyment of the countryside for many people. Other ideas include providing: a nature trail or paths suitable for wheelchair users, visually handicapped or elderly people; suitable access to viewpoints; an adapted bird or deer watching hide; or fishing platforms or pegs adapted for wheelchair users. Financial assistance may be available for some projects under the Countryside Stewardship scheme (eg for hard-surfaced paths for use by the disabled) or obtainable through the Country Landowners' Association Charitable Trust. Local authorities may know of other local charitable sources of funding.

Sources to contact for expert advice include the Fieldfare Trust, who are specifically concerned with access in the countryside for disabled people, and RADAR (the Royal Association for Disability and Rehabilitation) who publish a directory of countryside and wildlife sites for disabled people (see pages 75–77). The Countryside Commission's free advisory booklet *Informal countryside recreation for disabled people* (CCP 439), gives advice on the needs of various disability groups, suggests features and designs, and has a further extensive list of contact addresses. Highway authorities should also be able to suggest detailed designs for 'disabled friendly' gates, stiles and other features (designs have been published by the County Surveyors' Society).

Key points: Access for those with special needs

- Common features like stiles and poor path surfaces mean people whose mobility is impaired are severely restricted in the opportunities they have to enjoy the countryside.

- The local authority may ask you to cooperate with them in helping to develop routes that can be used by people with disabilities and others with special needs.

- Consider what you can do yourself to help to make suitable paths more accessible.

- Grants may be available to provide facilities for disabled people, but take specialist advice on whether your land is suitable and on what is needed.

- See pages 72–74 for sources of further information.

5. MANAGEMENT ISSUES AND PROBLEMS

Dealing with trespass

- People may trespass inadvertently while seeking to follow existing rights of way. This problem can be greatly reduced if rights of way are clearly waymarked, kept free of obstructions, and provided with gates or stiles where they cross fences, walls, etc.

- If a path is difficult to find, waymark the line with marker posts to ensure it is easy to follow. Further information is available in the Countryside Commission leaflet *Waymarking public rights of way* (CCP 246).

- Some users whom you consider to be trespassers may believe they have a right to use a particular route. If so, ask them to raise the issue with the highway authority, and to copy their evidence to you, so that their claim can be resolved.

- Use the procedures available under Section 31 (6) of the Highways Act 1980 to prevent a farm or estate track from becoming a public right of way through future use (see pages 24–27).

- Ensure that you, other members of your family and your employees are all aware of the public rights of way and roads across your land.

- You may ask trespassers to leave your property immediately or return to a public right of way. Allow them to do so freely.

- Keep a record of any damage, eg by taking photographs.

- If the same person persistently trespasses, you may apply to the county court for an injunction to prevent them continuing.

- Trespass by New Age Travellers, ravers, hunt saboteurs, or for illegal hare coursing, can cause particular difficulties. In such cases it is usually advisable to contact the police.

- You may use reasonable force to make trespassers leave if this is justified in the circumstances, but avoid this if possible. Use of excessive force could result in civil or criminal proceedings being taken against you or anyone acting on your behalf.

- If trespassers refuse to leave your property when asked, contact the police to discuss the circumstances and seek their advice.

- Avoid taking the law into your own hands if a serious confrontation occurs. Contact the police: they have powers to direct trespassers to leave in certain circumstances.

- See pages 5–6 for further information.

New Age Travellers

- Have up-to-date details of all your land to hand, eg maps and copies of title deeds and any tenancy or grazing agreements.
- Do not invite would-be trespassers onto your land.
- Consult your solicitor if you foresee a problem occurring. You may need to take out an injunction to prevent trespass. Make sure you can contact your solicitor quickly outside office hours.
- If you take preventative action (eg fencing off land or stopping-up an access with boulders or sand), take care not to obstruct public rights of way or other rights of access.
- You may take summary proceedings for possession; model forms are available from the NFU and CLA. An application to the court for a possession order may be made only by a person who is entitled to possession, which may not be the landowner where there is a tenant or lessee (your solicitor will be able to advise).
- New legislation, due to be introduced during 1994, will enable the police and local authorities to deal more effectively with New Age Travellers and other forms of trespass, eg unlicensed night-time rave parties and people disrupting lawful activities on land.
- Further advice is available from MAFF Regional Service Centres, the Home Office, the NFU and CLA.

Dogs

Worrying of livestock

- It is an offence under the Dogs (Protection of Livestock) Act 1953 to allow a dog to attack or chase livestock. When on enclosed land where there are sheep, dogs must be kept "on a lead or otherwise under close control".
- 'Close control' has not been defined, but a dog attacking any farm animal would clearly be out of control, and you could shoot the dog if there was no other way of stopping it. Any such action must be reported to the local police within 48 hours.
- Whenever possible, approach the owner of the dog that is causing problems. If necessary you can report the owner to the police and ask them to prosecute. Compensation may also be claimed from the dog owner.

- You can ask your local authority to make an order under Section 27 of the Road Traffic Act 1988 requiring dogs to be kept on leads on specific rights of way.
- If an order is made you can put up notices insisting "Dogs must be kept on a lead at all times on this path". Talk to your local authority about steps you can take to enforce this.
- If the authority is unwilling to make an order you can put up notices asking owners to control their dogs, eg "Please keep your dog on a lead" or stating "Dogs must be kept under close control".

Fouling by dogs

- Dog owners may be willing to pay for an annual licence to exercise their dogs in a 'fido field'. Consider setting aside an area in one of your least productive fields for this purpose.
- The Environmental Health Officer of your local district council may be able to offer advice on combating dog fouling.
- 'Poop-scoop' byelaws can be made by the local authority under Section 86 of the Environmental Protection Act 1990, and the Litter (Animal Droppings) Order 1991, to require owners to clear up after their dogs, eg in village streets or confined rights of way, but not in the open countryside.

Your own dogs

- Farm dogs must also be kept under control. A landowner who kept several dogs behind a fence alongside a public footpath was recently prosecuted under Section 3(1) of the Dangerous Dogs Act 1991. The dogs had been behaving aggressively, intimidating walkers. The owner was fined £416 and the local authority was awarded costs of £300.

Crop spraying

- In general, public rights of way and other highways should not be oversprayed: pesticides (including herbicides) should be confined to the adjacent crop. Spraying paths can endanger people and animals and is wasteful.
- If the product label states that people and animals should stay out of a treated crop, you should place warning signs at all points where paths enter the sprayed area, including any points where people pick wild fruit. The signs should say "Sprayed: please keep to the path" and be left in place until it is safe to remove them.

- You should cease spraying immediately if anyone steps onto a path which crosses or adjoins a field that is being sprayed. Allow them adequate time to get clear before recommencing spraying.
- Some herbicides are approved for use in killing vegetation growing on public rights of way (eg crop seedlings growing on a cross-field path which has been cultivated and restored). Before using any spray for this purpose you should check the product label. In general it is better to cut such vegetation than to kill it by spraying.
- Further guidance is available from MAFF and the Health and Safety Executive (HSE). See, in particular, the *Code of practice for the safe use of pesticides on farms and holdings* (HMSO, £5).

Cycling

- Cyclists are permitted to ride any pedal cycle, including 'mountain bikes', on bridleways, byways open to all traffic and roads used as public paths (where these have not yet been reclassified).
- The permission granted under Section 30 of the Countryside Act 1968 for cyclists to ride on bridleways is subject to the condition that they give way to walkers and horse-riders.
- Cyclists do not have a right to ride on footpaths. Landowners may sue someone who does so for trespass, or take out an injunction against a persistent offender.
- The highway authority may also be prepared to take action against such trespass where the path surface is being damaged.
- Contact user groups, eg the British Mountain Bike Federation (BMBF) and Cyclists' Touring Club, for help in reducing problems. Groups such as the BMBF produce their own Codes of Conduct for riders.
- Consider dedicating a public footpath as a bridleway to regularise public use where the path is suitable or its creation as a bridleway will create a circular route. Discuss this with the highway authority and user groups.

Motor vehicles

- Motorised vehicles may be driven on public roads (whether surfaced or not), byways open to all traffic and many roads used as public paths. But they must be licensed, taxed and insured, and driven carefully, as they would on any other highway.

- It is an offence under Section 34 of the Road Traffic Act 1988 to ride a motorcycle or drive a motor vehicle without permission on a footpath, bridleway, or on any land which is not a road.

- Make sure you know what public rights exist over your land: check the definitive map and statement and the list of streets maintainable at public expense. Both sets of records are held by the highway authority (see pages 15–21).

- If disagreements arise over whether vehicular rights exist over a particular track, first check the position with the highway authority. If necessary, ask vehicle users to submit their evidence to the highway authority, and to copy it to you, so that the situation can be clarified.

- The national vehicle user organisations have codes of conduct and are keen to promote responsible use. Their members will produce their membership cards if asked to do so. The organisations can be contacted through the Motoring Organisations' Land Access and Recreation Association.

- Combined action is often the most effective way of combating problems of illegal or irresponsible use by vehicles, or of resolving the conflict that can sometimes arise even when vehicles are used entirely legally and responsibly:
  - **Vehicle clubs** can police their own members; help to reduce incidents of misuse by non-members; and voluntarily agree to restrain use (eg avoiding use in winter or limiting the types or numbers of vehicles);
  - **The local authority** can promote understanding of everyone's rights and responsibilities; repair surface damage where it occurs; and require vehicle owners who were responsible for such damage (where this can be proved) to contribute to the costs;
  - **The police** can deal with unlicensed vehicles or reckless driving;
  - **Landowners and farmers** can keep a log, record registration numbers or take photographs to help the police or authority identify those responsible; provide other areas where vehicles can be used without causing damage or conflict (but see the advice on pages 54–57); and avoid damaging tracks by their own use (eg not using heavy farm machinery on unsurfaced, clay tracks in wet weather).

- If, despite these measures, use by vehicles remains a serious problem, the highway authority may be persuaded to make a Traffic Regulation Order under the Road Traffic Regulation Act 1984 to restrict or prohibit use. Substantial evidence will be needed to justify it.

Mike Williams/CC

Promoted routes

- If you feel that a guide book is wrong or misleading ask users to give you the names of its author and publisher.

- Check the guide book against the definitive map. Ask the highway authority to investigate any discrepancies.

- The Outdoor Writers' Guild recognises that promoting routes can cause problems, especially if the routes are not on a definitive map. It is developing a code of good practice for guide book writers.

- Submit a map, statement and declaration to the highway authority under Section 31 (6) of the Highways Act 1980 (see pages 24–27).

- Ensure that all public rights of way are indicated by signposts where they leave the metalled roads and are properly waymarked along their length.

Sponsored events or competitions

- Many organisers of sponsored events or competitions using public rights of way will contact the local authority beforehand.

- Some organisers will even take the trouble to contact individual landowners along the route, although on long walks this is often impractical.

- Some sponsored walks or rides may be considered a 'public procession' under Section 11 of the Public Order Act, 1986 and require police consent.
- The Ramblers' Association, NFU and the Long Distance Walkers Association both produce codes of practice for sponsored walks or events.
- Ask local authorities and the police to encourage walk organisers to follow published codes of practice.
- Encourage organisers to publicise planned events or competitive events through local farming newsletters, or in the local press, well in advance.

Gates and stiles

- Seek consent from the highway authority under Section 147 of the Highways Act 1980 before erecting any stile or gate across a public right of way, or replacing one with the other.
- The Country Code asks users to 'Fasten all gates'. Fixing notices to gates to this effect can help avoid problems of stock straying. Make sure that your gates open and shut easily so there is no excuse for them being left open; fit self-closing fasteners on gates.
- Ensure that gates on bridleways can be negotiated by riders, preferably without having to dismount. Ask the highway authority for advice on suitable fastening devices.
- In some locations, you could provide a stile alongside a gate. Avoid inconveniencing users: a stile may be acceptable on a moorland path used by young, fit walkers, but erecting one on a village path could prevent use by the elderly. Always seek prior permission from the highway authority.
- Where necessary fit 'dog-latches' to stiles to help avoid damage to stiles or mesh fences. The latches can be lifted to allow a dog through and then dropped to keep the stile stock-proof. The highway authority will be able to advise on suitable designs or may supply and fit dog-latches.
- Where appropriate, replace step stiles with squeeze stiles or gates, or install gates in fences instead of stiles, to help make access easier for the elderly, less fit or users of pushchairs. Always seek prior permission from the highway authority.
- A minimum contribution of 25 per cent of the costs of any works to gates and stiles on a public right of way may be claimed by the occupier from the highway authority. Some authorities provide materials, eg stile kits, and others may carry out the work themselves.

Fences

- Public rights of way cannot be legally diverted temporarily to erect fencing.
- Obtain permission from the highway authority before erecting fences of any sort across a public right of way, even if only temporary.
- Barbed wire fences should always have the wire fastened on the side of the posts facing away from the right of way. Ensure that there is no barbed wire on gates which need to be opened or on posts which users might hold onto for support.
- Avoid siting electric fences alongside bridleways and byways: horses can bolt if they touch them.
- Barbed wire fences alongside narrow rights of way can constitute a nuisance.
- Use barbless wire or timber in fences wherever possible near rights of way.

Litter

- It is an offence under Section 87 of the Environmental Protection Act 1990 to dump rubbish other than at an authorised tip.
- Landowners are responsible for clearing litter from their own property, whoever put it there: seek advice from the Environmental Health Officer of your local district council.
- Local authorities can require litter and rubbish which constitutes a nuisance to be removed from public rights of way under Section 149 of the Highways Act 1980.
- Report fly-tipping or other pollution of watercourses to the National Rivers Authority on its Freephone Emergency Hotline: 0800 807060.
- Some authorities may help people to remove rubbish, particularly large items such as abandoned vehicles.
- Businesses which transport waste may be required to obtain a licence or risk prosecution.
- Further advice is available from the Department of Environment.

Car parking

- Motorists do not need to seek permission from the adjacent landowner to park their vehicles on the highway: doing so is incidental to the right to pass and repass. Motorists must not obstruct the highway or any exit onto it.

- Grass verges are usually part of the highway. Again, no permission is needed to park on them. Placing stones or other obstructions to prevent parking on road verges which are not privately owned but form part of the highway is illegal and potentially dangerous. Any concerns over parking on road verges should be discussed with the highway authority and police. Both may be able to offer advice and assistance.

- Polite notices, for example "No parking — gate in use", can be used to discourage parking in front of gates. The notices can be permanent or put up a day or so before you need to use a particular gate.

- You could provide a car park at certain times of the year if the demand exists, for example near a local beauty spot. Check with the planning department of your district council to find out whether planning permission is required.

- Landowners may take on responsibility from the highway authority for managing highway verges adjacent to their property under agreements under Section 142 of the Highways Act 1980.

Shooting and carrying firearms

- It is an offence, under Section 19 of the Firearms Act 1968, for anyone other than the landowner or occupier (or someone with their permission) to carry a loaded firearm or air gun, or any unloaded one with ammunition, in a public place (including a public highway). This also applies to anything that has a blade or is sharply pointed (other than a small folding pocket-knife) or is made or adapted for use as an offensive weapon.

- It is an offence under Section 161 of the Highways Act 1980 to fire a gun within 15 metres (50 feet) of the centre of a road or byway open to all traffic if any highway user is injured, interrupted or endangered as a result.

- Never shoot across or near a public right of way when it is being used: this could amount to a common law nuisance, wilful obstruction, intimidation or a breach of the Health and Safety at Work etc. Act 1974. Such an action could well result in the loss of a gun licence.

- Check whether a right of way exists on or near any area where shooting is to occur. Be aware of path users; cease shooting as they pass and let them get well clear before starting again.

- Do not attempt to divert a public right of way temporarily during a shoot: this is illegal and you cannot prevent people using the definitive path if they wish.

- Consider creating a new public right of way to help to reduce conflict on shooting days and disturbance to game.

- If people are trespassing off a right of way into a shoot, you can waymark the path, or erect notices or fencing.

- On moorland or in woodland consider an access agreement to provide public access at certain times of the year, but excluding the sensitive periods of game management.

Charles Meecham/CC

Poaching and disturbance of wildlife

- If confronted by suspected poachers first assess the seriousness of the situation. If the people involved are not threatening, simply ask them to leave your property and point out that they may be committing an offence.

- If you are in any doubt as to the potential danger, you should call the police immediately: do not take matters into your own hands.

- Where fisheries are involved contact the National Rivers Authority. Poaching incidents can be reported on its Freephone Emergency Hotline: 0800 807060.

- It is illegal to dig for badgers, steal eggs or disturb wild birds (other than recognised pests) during the nesting season.

- Contact your local police headquarters. They may have a Wildlife or Environment Liaison Officer. Give as much information as you can about any suspicious activity.

- You can also ask English Nature for advice. If birds are involved, you can also contact the Royal Society for the Protection of Birds.

- Report any suspected incidents of illegal poisoning of wildlife and animals and domestic animals to the Ministry of Agriculture, Fisheries and Food on its Freephone Hotline: 0800 321600.

Metal detecting

- Disturbing the ground or removing objects without the owner's permission may be trespass, criminal damage or theft. Metal detecting on a public right of way is a trespass.

- On the site of a scheduled ancient monument or area of archaeological importance it is an offence under Section 42 of the Ancient Monuments and Archaeological Areas Act 1979 to use a metal detector to detect or locate objects of archaeological or historical interest without written permission from the Secretary of State for National Heritage.

- Challenge alleged offenders and report them to the police as necessary.

- Report any infringements on archaeological sites to English Heritage.

- Contact the National Council for Metal Detecting for advice. It has a code of practice for its members.

- Negotiate a formal written agreement with local groups or individuals. The CLA and NFU publish model agreements.

Fruit picking

- Respect local customs unless they cause you serious problems. You could restrict access by erecting notices in sensitive locations.

- People who pick wild mushrooms or fruit from plants growing wild (eg blackberries) on any land are guilty of theft under Section 4 of the Theft Act 1968 **only** if they do so for commercial purposes.
- People who pick, uproot or destroy wild plants without the permission of the landowner may be guilty of an offence under the Wildlife and Countryside Act 1981.
- Report anyone who is picking fruit for profit from your land without permission to the police.

Woodland management

- You should check the condition of trees on your land adjacent to public rights of way periodically, to ensure that they pose no danger to the public.
- Voluntary 'Tree Wardens' have been appointed in many areas. You can contact them (usually through the district council) for advice on checking the condition of trees and on appropriate action to deal with hazards.
- When felling trees near public rights of way, always be aware of your responsibilities to the public under the Health and Safety at Work etc. Act 1974.
- Always ensure that permission to fell trees has been obtained from the Forestry Commission (a felling licence may be necessary) and the district council (if trees are covered by a Tree Preservation Order or are within a Conservation Area).
- Warning signs should be erected at any points of entry into a woodland where deer are being culled. To avoid public concern these could briefly explain that deer need to be culled for the benefit of the woodland.

Bulls

- Ensure that bulls are not kept in a field crossed by a path unless they do not exceed 10 months old or are both not of a recognised dairy breed and are accompanied by cows or heifers. Breeds of bull which must not be kept in fields with a public right of way are Ayrshire, British Friesian, British Holstein, Dairy Shorthorn, Guernsey, Jersey and Kerry.
- Follow the advice in the Health and Safety Executive Guidance Note GS35 on the *Safe custody and handling of bulls on farms and similar premises*. Warning notices should be displayed **only** when a bull is present in a field.

- **Never** keep an animal known to be aggressive (including any bull of whatever breed) in a field to which the public has any access.

Theft

- Contact your local Police Crime Prevention Officer for advice on securing your premises and discouraging crime.
- Ensure that, wherever possible, machinery and implements are locked away, especially portable items such as chainsaws.
- Many police forces organise schemes to help tackle particular forms of crime: Neighbourhood Watch, Country Watch, Farm Watch, Horse Watch, and Poacher Watch provide examples. Ask your local Police Crime Prevention Officer for advice.
- As a rule, those intent on theft will make use of any means of access to a target site, regardless of whether or not a particular path is a public right of way. Report anyone behaving suspiciously to the police.
- Improved security measures are likely to be far more effective than diverting a public right of way away from farm or estate buildings. Thieves can be deterred where paths are well-used. Walkers, riders and motor vehicle users can play an important role in reporting suspicious behaviour.

USEFUL PUBLICATIONS

Statutes and Circulars:

Firearms Act 1968.

Theft Act 1968.

Health and Safety at Work etc. Act 1974.

Ancient Monuments and Archaeological Areas Act 1979.

Highways Act 1980 (As amended).

Wildlife and Countryside Act 1981 (As amended).

Road Traffic Regulation Act 1984.

Public Order Act 1986.

Environmental Protection Act 1990.

Rights of Way Act 1990 (Amended the Highways Act 1980).

Dangerous Dogs Act 1991.

Public Rights of Way. DOE Circular 2/93.

Recovery of Costs of Public Path and Rail Crossing Orders. DOE Circular 3/93.

Available from: HMSO Publications, PO Box 276, London, SW8 5DT. Telephone Enquiries: 071 873 0011. (Telephone orders: 071 873 9090).

Countryside Commission:

Countryside Stewardship : Handbook and application pack (CCP 453), revised 1994.

A guide to procedures for public path orders (CCP 449), 1994.

A guide to definitive map procedures (CCP 285), revised 1992.

Waymarking public rights of way (CCP 246), revised 1992.

Out in the country: Where you can go and what you can do (CCP 186), revised 1992.

The Rights of Way Act 1990: Guidance notes for farmers (CCP 299), 1990.

Horses in the countryside (CCP 261), revised 1993.

Informal countryside recreation for disabled people: A practical guide for countryside managers (CCP 439), 1994.

Available from: Countryside Commission, Postal Sales, PO Box 124, Walgrave, Northampton, NN6 9TL (Tel: 0604 781848).

Sports Council:

A countryside for sport: a policy for sport and recreation, 1992.

District sport and recreation strategies: A guide, 1991.

Available from: The Sports Council, 16 Upper Woburn Place, London, WC1H 0QP (Tel: 071 388 1277).

Rights of Way Review Committee:

PGN 1: Proposed changes to rights of way and definitive maps: A code of practice on consultation

PGN 2: Deemed dedication of rights of way: Section 31(6) of the Highways Act 1980

PGN 3: Minimising objections to definitive map modification orders and reclassification orders

PGN 4: Securing agreement to public path orders.

Available from: The Secretary, Rights of Way Review Committee, 1/5 Wandsworth Road, London, SW8 2XX. (Tel: 071 582 6878).

Country Landowners' Association:

Public Rights of Way: Rebutting Deemed Dedication (A2/93), 1993.

Commons (L6/92), 1992.

Environmental Land Management Services (E2/91), 1991.

Land Opportunities for the 1990s: a Handbook of Alternative Enterprises, 1991.

Occupiers' Liability, 1993. (Joint leaflet with the British Mountaineering Council).

Further handbooks are in preparation.

Available from: Publications Manager, Country Landowners' Association, 16 Belgrave Square, London, SW1X 8PQ (Tel: 071 235 0511).

National Farmers' Union:

Rights of Way : A checklist for farmers. Advisory leaflet.

Sport and recreation on the farm.

Sponsored walks in the countryside : A handbook for organisers.

Available from: National Farmers' Union, 22 Long Acre, London, WC2E 9LY (Tel: 071 235 5077).

MAFF:

Trespass : Advice for farmers and landowners. (Available from MAFF Regional Service Centres).

A Farmers Guide to the Planning System, 1992. (Available free from Department of the Environment, PO Box 151, London, E15 2HF).

Success with sporting enterprises on farms.

Success with farm-based tourist accommodation.

Success with farm diversification.

Success with marketing farm diversification enterprises.

Available from: MAFF Publications, London, SE99 7TP. (Tel: 081 694 8862).

Forestry Commission:

Woodland Grant Scheme Applicant's Pack.

Available from: Forestry Commission, Grants and Licences Division, 231 Corstorphine Road, Edinburgh, EH12 7AT. (Tel: 031 334 0303).

Open Spaces Society:

Our common land : The law and history of commons and village greens. P. Clayden, 1992. (£9.50).

Rights of Way: A guide to law and practice. J. Riddall and J. Trevelyan, 1992. (£14.00). (Joint publication with the Ramblers' Association).

Our common right: The story of common land. (50p).

Available from: Open Spaces Society, 25A Bell Street, Henley on Thames, Oxon, RG9 2BA. (Tel: 0491 573535).

USEFUL ADDRESSES

Amber Valley Farm Rides, Groundwork Amber Valley, 19 Bridge Street, Belper, Derbyshire DE56 1AY. Tel: 0773 824588.

British Horse Society (BHS), British Equestrian Centre, Stoneleigh, Kenilworth, Warwickshire CV8 2LR. Tel: 0203 696697.

British Mountain Bike Federation (BMBF), 36 Rockingham Road, Kettering, Northamptonshire NN16 8HG. Tel: 0536 412211.

British Mountaineering Council (BMC), Crawford House, Precinct Centre, Booth Street East, Manchester M13 9RZ. Tel: 061 273 5835.

British Orienteering Federation, 'Riversdale', Dale Road North, Darley Dale, Matlock, Derbyshire DE4 2HX.

British Trust for Conservation Volunteers (BTCV), 36 St. Mary's Street, Wallingford, Oxon OX10 0EU. Tel: 0491 39766.

Byways and Bridleways Trust (BBT), The Granary, Charlcutt, Calne, Wiltshire SN11 9HL. Tel: 0249 740273.

Central Council of Physical Recreation, Francis House, Francis Street, London SW1P 1DE. Tel: 071 828 3163.

CLA Charitable Trust, c/o 16 Belgrave Square, London SW1X 8PQ. Tel: 071 235 0511.

Council for British Archaeology (CBA), Bowes Morrell House, 111 Walmgate, York YO1 2UA. Tel: 0904 671417.

Council for the Protection of Rural England (CPRE), Warwick House, 25 Buckingham Palace Road, London SW1W 0PP. Tel: 071 976 6433.

Country Landowners' Association (CLA), 16 Belgrave Square, London SW1X 8PQ. Tel: 071 235 0511.

Countryside Commission, John Dower House, Crescent Place, Cheltenham, Gloucestershire GL50 3RA. Tel: 0242 521381.

Country Trust, Stratford Grange, Stratford St Andrew, Saxmundham, Suffolk IP17 1LF. Tel: 0728 604818.

Cyclists' Touring Club (CTC), 69 Meadrow, Godalming, Surrey GU7 3HS. Tel: 0483 417217.

Department of the Environment, Directorate of Rural Affairs, Tollgate House, Houlton Street, Bristol BS2 9DJ. Tel: 0272 878000.

Department of Transport, 2 Marsham Street, London SW1P 3EB.

East Anglian Farm Rides, Highfield Farm, Kelvedon, Essex CO5 9BJ. Tel: 0206 251790.

English Heritage, Fortress House, 23 Savile Row, London W1X 1AB. Tel: 071 973 3000.

English Nature, Northminster House, Peterborough PE1 1UA. Tel: 0733 340345.

English Tourist Board, Thames Tower, Black's Road, London W6 9EL. Tel: 071 846 9000.

Fieldfare Trust, 67a The Wicker, Sheffield S3 8HT.

Forestry Commission, 231 Corstophine Road, Edinburgh EH12 7AT. Tel: 031 334 0303.

Forestry Trust for Conservation and Education, The Old Estate Office, Englefield Road, Theale, Reading, Berkshire RG7 5DZ. Tel 0734 323523.

Groundwork Foundation, 85/87 Cornwall Street, Birmingham B3 3BY. Tel: 021 236 8565. (Umbrella body for Local Groundwork Trusts).

Health and Safety Executive (HSE), Public Enquiry Point, Broad Lane, Sheffield S3 7HQ. Tel: 0742 892345.

Institute of Public Rights of Way Officers, c/o The Secretary, Claire Foster, 25 Church Street, Holloway, Matlock, Derbyshire DE4 5AY.

Long Distance Walkers' Association, c/o Brian Smith, 10 Temple Park Close, Leeds LS15 0JJ. Tel: 0532 642255.

Ministry of Agriculture, Conservation Policy Division, Nobel House, 17 Smith Square, London SW1P 3HX. Tel: 071 238 3000. MAFF Freephone Illegal Poisoning Hotline: Tel: 0800 321600.

Motoring Organisations' Land Access and Recreation Association (LARA): Motor Recreation Development Officer: PO Box 19, Newcastle upon Tyne NE3 5HW; Motor Sport Development Officer: c/o Auto-Cycle Union, Wood Street, Rugby, Warwickshire CV21 2YX.

National Council for Metal Detecting, 3 Riverside Mews, Park Road, Nantwich, Cheshire CW5 7AG.

National Farmers' Union (NFU), 22 Long Acre, London WC2E 9LY. Tel: 071 235 5077.

National Federation of Young Farmers' Club (NFYFC), National Agricultural Centre, Stoneleigh, Kenilworth, Warwickshire CV8 2LG. Tel: 0203 696544.

National Forest Development Team, Stanleigh House, Chapel Street, Donisthorpe, Derbyshire DE12 7PS. Tel: 0530 273816.

The National Gardens Scheme Charitable Trust, Hatchlands Park, East Clandon, Guildford, Surrey GU4 7RT.

National Rivers Authority, Rivers House, Waterside Drive, Aztec West, Almondsbury, Bristol BS12 4UD. Tel: 0454 624400. NRA Freephone Emergency Hotline: Tel: 0800 807060.

Old Down Toll Rides, 13 Denys Court, Olveston, Bristol BS12 3DW. Tel: 0454 616752.

Open Spaces Society, 25a Bell Street, Henley on Thames, Oxon RG9 2BA. Tel: 0491 573535.

Ordnance Survey, Romsey Road, Maybush, Southampton SO9 3DH. Tel: 0703 792000.

Outdoor Writers' Guild, Acting Secretary, 27 Camwood, Clayton Green, Bamber Bridge, Preston, Lancs PR5 8LA.

Ramblers' Association (RA), 1/5 Wandsworth Road, London SW8 2XX. Tel: 071 582 6878.

Rights of Way Review Committee, c/o Ramblers' Association, 1/5 Wandsworth Road, London SW8 2XX. Tel: 071 582 6878.

Royal Association for Disability and Rehabilitation (RADAR), 12 City Forum, 250 City Road, London EC1V 8AF. Tel: 071 250 3222.

Royal Society for the Protection of Birds (RSPB), The Lodge, Sandy, Bedfordshire SG19 2DL. Tel: 0767 680551.

South-Eastern Toll-Rides, Long Acres Farm, Newchapel Road, Lingfield, Surrey RH7 6LE. Tel: 0342 834307.

Sports Council, 16 Upper Woburn Place, London WC1H 0QP. Tel: 071 388 1277.

Woodland Trust, Autumn Park, Dysart Road, Grantham, Lincolnshire NG31 6LL. Tel: 0476 74297.

And, wherever you go, follow the Country Code

- Enjoy the countryside and respect its life and work.
- Guard against all risk of fire.
- Fasten all gates.
- Keep your dogs under close control.
- Keep to public paths across farmland.
- Use gates and stiles to cross fences, hedges and walls.
- Leave livestock, crops and machinery alone.
- Take your litter home.
- Help to keep all water clean.
- Protect wildlife, plants and trees.
- Take special care on country roads.
- Make no unnecessary noise.